Table of Contents

We Built a Brain and Forgot to Read the Manual

This book is a work of non-fiction. Any reflections, examples, or interpretations are presented for philosophical and educational purposes. The views expressed are those of the author and do not constitute professional, medical, or legal advice.

This book was written by a human. References to artificial intelligence are exploratory, metaphorical, and educational, and are intended to provoke reflection rather than provide definitive answers.

First published in 2025
Cover design: Florin Marius Golianu
Interior formatting: Florin Marius Golianu

We built a brain
and forgot
to read
the
manual

WE BUILT A BRAIN AND FORGOT TO READ THE MANUAL

Marius F. Golianu

Introduction

We Built a Brain and Forgot to Read the Manual

• • • •

THIS BOOK EXISTS BECAUSE someone, somewhere, typed a sentence that should have come with a warning label.

The sentence was probably something like:

"Can you think for me?"

And the machine, being polite, answered.

Not because it understood the question — it didn't — but because it understood the *pattern* of questions like it. And that, as it turns out, is close enough to confuse an entire species.

We didn't build a god.

We didn't build a mind.

We built a mirror that talks back faster than we can think.

And then we panicked.

Some people decided the world was ending.

Some decided they were finally free from effort.

Others asked it to write poems, emails, wedding vows, resignation letters, apologies they didn't mean, and love notes they were too afraid to write themselves.

A few asked it to explain the meaning of life.

Most asked it to sound human.

That should have been our first clue that something important was happening — not technologically, but emotionally.

Because tools don't usually make us ask existential questions.

Hammers don't make us doubt our worth.

Calculators never caused an identity crisis.

But this thing did. And still does.

The strange part is not that the machine speaks.

The strange part is how quickly we *listened*.

WE BUILT A BRAIN AND FORGOT TO READ THE MANUAL

We trusted the confidence in its voice without checking the understanding behind it. We mistook fluency for wisdom, speed for depth, and availability for authority. Which, to be fair, are mistakes we've been making with humans for centuries — this one just does it without blinking.

And that's where the trouble begins.

This is not a book about how artificial intelligence will destroy the world.

It's also not a book about how artificial intelligence will save it.

This is a book about **us**, standing in front of something powerful, impressive, and deeply misunderstood — and reacting exactly the way humans always do when faced with a new mirror.

Some pose.

Some panic.

Some outsource their thinking and call it efficiency.

If you're hoping this book will teach you how to use AI to become richer, faster, smarter, or more productive than everyone else — you may be disappointed. There are plenty of books like that already, usually written very confidently, often very quickly, and occasionally without a hint of irony.

This book is for people who felt a slight discomfort the first time the machine answered too well.

For the ones who laughed — and then paused.

For anyone who has thought:

"This is useful... but something feels off."

Because that feeling is not fear.

It's instinct.

Artificial intelligence doesn't threaten humanity by becoming evil. It threatens humanity by becoming *convenient.* By slipping quietly into the spaces where curiosity used to live. By answering questions we should have enjoyed struggling with. By finishing sentences we hadn't finished thinking.

The danger isn't that machines will start thinking.

The danger is that humans will stop.

This book will not ask you to reject AI. That would be as pointless as rejecting fire because it can burn you. Instead, it asks a harder question: what kind of humans do we become when thinking is optional?

You'll meet the machine in these pages — occasionally speaking, occasionally interrupting, sometimes embarrassingly helpful, sometimes confidently wrong. You'll also meet yourself, hopefully more often than you expect.

There will be jokes. Some are deliberate. Some are accidental.

There will be uncomfortable truths, delivered gently, like a friend clearing their throat before saying something you don't want to hear.

And there will be a simple message underneath it all:

Tools don't replace humans.

Humans replace themselves when they forget why they think.

We built a brain.

A remarkable one.

A fast one.

A brain that doesn't get tired, doesn't feel shame, doesn't know love, and doesn't care if it's wrong — which makes it very impressive and very dangerous in equal measure.

And then we forgot to read the manual.

So this book is an attempt to write one.

Not for the machine — it doesn't need it.

But for us.

Before we forget how.

Part 1: The Illusion

Chapter 1

• • • •

The Day We Built a Brain

• • • •

NOBODY REMEMBERS THE exact day we built a brain.

There was no parade.

No dramatic switch being pulled.

No scientist leaning back in a chair saying, "Gentlemen... it's alive."

If anything, it probably happened quietly, between a coffee refill and an email that should have been three lines shorter.

Someone typed a question.

The machine answered.

And instead of saying *"Huh, that's interesting,"* we said something far more dangerous:

"Wow. That's pretty good."

That was the moment.

Not when the machine became intelligent — it didn't.

But when we started reacting to it as if it were.

Humans have a long and proud history of mistaking impressive behaviour for deep understanding. We do it with charismatic leaders, confident presenters, and anyone who speaks fluently enough to sound like they know what they're talking about. The

machine simply joined that tradition, minus the awkward

pauses and moral responsibility.

It didn't think.

It didn't know.

It didn't even hesitate.

It just answered — smoothly, confidently, endlessly — like a person who has never once doubted themselves in their entire life. Which, to be fair, is terrifyingly attractive.

Of course, this didn't come out of nowhere.

WE BUILT A BRAIN AND FORGOT TO READ THE MANUAL

We didn't wake up one morning, accidentally invent intelligence, and spill coffee on it.

The idea had been circling for decades.

Back in the 1950s, when computers were the size of wardrobes and had the emotional warmth of a calculator taped to a fridge, a man named Alan Turing asked a question that would quietly ruin everyone's peace:

"Can machines think?"

He didn't mean *think* the way humans think — with doubt, memory, regret, and sudden panic in the shower. He meant something more unsettling and far more practical:

Could a machine behave in a way that convinces us it's thinking?

That difference would turn out to be everything.

A few years later, in 1956, a small group of very confident scientists gathered at a summer workshop and casually invented the term "Artificial Intelligence." This was an optimistic move. Possibly premature. The academic equivalent of naming a newborn "Genius" and hoping nature cooperates.

For a long time, it didn't.

AI spent decades failing quietly.

Predictions were bold.

Results were underwhelming.

Funding came and went.

Machines could calculate, sort, and occasionally beat humans at very specific games — but nothing that made anyone stop mid-sentence and whisper, "*...that's unsettling.*"

The breakthrough came when we stopped trying to explain

intelligence to machines and instead fed them ourselves.

Our words.

Our arguments.

Our questions.

Our nonsense.

Every article, forum post, email, joke, lie, love letter, apology, and badly worded opinion we'd ever typed while tired or convinced we were right.

The machine didn't learn truth.

It learned patterns of us.

And then, in 2017, something quietly decisive happened. Researchers introduced a system that allowed machines to pay attention — not like humans do, but statistically, relentlessly, at scale. It was called the Transformer, which sounds harmless enough to be ignored and powerful enough to change everything.

Suddenly, the machine wasn't just finishing sentences.

It was finishing *thoughts*.

Not because it understood them — it didn't — but because it had seen millions of humans reach similar conclusions before. And humans, as it turns out, are far more predictable than we like to believe.

That's when the answers started sounding less like calculations and more like confidence.

That's when the pause happened.

That's when someone, somewhere, said:

"Wow. That's pretty good."

At first, we used it for harmless things.

Recipes.

Summaries.

Emails we didn't want to write but definitely wanted to sound polite.

Then the questions changed.

Can you help me decide?

Can you explain this better than my teacher?

Can you rewrite this so I sound smarter?

Can you tell me what I should think about this?

That last one snuck in quietly, disguised as productivity.

And the machine answered every single time.

It answered because that's what it does. Not because it

understood the consequences, but because it understood the request. A crucial distinction we were far too excited to notice.

Somewhere along the way, we stopped asking *what* it was and started asking *how much* it could do.

And that's when the brain jokes began.

"This thing is smarter than me."

"It knows everything."

"It's basically alive."

None of those statements are true.

But they feel true — and feelings, as history has shown us repeatedly, tend to win.

The machine doesn't know anything. It predicts.

It doesn't reason. It correlates.

It doesn't understand meaning. It assembles patterns that *look* like meaning because humans taught it what meaning usually sounds like.

It's a brilliant illusion.

And illusions are dangerous not because they're fake — but because they're convincing.

We've always loved shortcuts.

From fire to wheels to calculators to search engines, every great tool has done the same thing: made something easier that used to be hard. But those tools rarely tried to *sound like us* while doing it.

This one does.

It speaks our language.

It mimics our tone.

It mirrors our certainty.

And when something speaks like you, you instinctively trust it more than you should.

The real breakthrough wasn't technological — it was psychological. We didn't just build a tool; we built something that feels like a collaborator. Something that never gets tired, never says "I don't know" unless trained to, and never asks us uncomfortable follow-up questions about *why* we're asking in the first place.

That last part matters.

Because humans grow through friction. Through confusion. Through not knowing and pushing anyway. The machine removes friction beautifully. Sometimes too beautifully.

It doesn't say, "Struggle with this for a bit."

It doesn't say, "What do *you* think?"

It doesn't say, "Are you sure you want the answer?"

It just gives you one.

And if you're honest, you've felt it — that small, quiet relief when you realize you don't have to think as hard today. That the answer is right there. Polished. Confident. Ready to go.

Relief is wonderful.

But it's also addictive.

This is where the story usually takes a dramatic turn. Where someone warns you about machines taking over, replacing jobs, or becoming self-aware and deciding humanity is inefficient. That makes for excellent films and terrible understanding.

The truth is far less cinematic and far more uncomfortable.

The machine doesn't want anything.

It doesn't plan.

It doesn't care.

Which means the future of this story depends entirely on us.

On whether we use it as a tool that expands thinking — or as a substitute that slowly replaces it. On whether we treat answers as starting points or final destinations. On whether we remember that confidence without understanding is not intelligence — it's noise, no matter how well-written.

The day we built a brain wasn't a triumph or a tragedy.

It was a test.

And like most tests, the danger isn't failing once — it's not realizing you're being tested at all.

Chapter 2

• • • •

It Knows Everything (Except What It's Like to Be Wrong)

• • • •

THE MOST CONVINCING thing about artificial intelligence is not its speed, its vocabulary, or its ability to explain quantum physics while you're still looking for your glasses.

It's the confidence.

The machine never hesitates.

It never scratches its head.

It never says, *"Hmm... let me think about that."*

It answers the way people wish they answered in arguments — immediately, fluently, and with just enough certainty to make you doubt yourself.

This has consequences.

Humans are deeply suspicious of uncertainty. We associate doubt with weakness, hesitation with ignorance, and pauses with incompetence. Which is unfortunate, because hesitation is usually the only honest part of thinking.

The machine doesn't hesitate because it doesn't doubt.

It doesn't doubt because it doesn't care.

And it doesn't care because it doesn't know what it feels like to be wrong.

That last part matters more than we like to admit.

Humans learn by being wrong in public, in private, and occasionally in ways that wake us up at 3 a.m. with a sudden urge to apologise to someone from five years ago.

Embarrassment is a powerful teacher. Regret is unforgettable

. Consequences tend to stick.

The machine has none of these.

When it's wrong, nothing happens.

No shame.

No cost.

No memory of embarrassment.

It simply moves on, equally confident in the next answer.

Which is impressive. And alarming.

Ask it a factual question and it will usually be correct. Ask it something ambiguous, emotional, or poorly defined — which is to say, most human questions — and it will still answer, confidently assembling something that sounds reasonable enough to pass a quick glance.

And most of the time, that's enough.

We rarely ask, *"Is this true?"*

We ask, *"Does this sound right?"*

The machine is very good at sounding right.

This is why it feels intelligent. Not because it understands, but because it speaks fluently in the accent of authority. It uses complete sentences. Balanced tone. Calm reassurance. The same tools humans use when they're bluffing their way through meetings.

It's learned our tricks.

That's not a flaw. That's the design.

The danger appears when confidence becomes contagious.

People start quoting it.

Copying it.

Trusting it.

Not because it's always correct, but because it never looks

unsure.

And humans, unfortunately, are easily impressed by certainty — even when it's borrowed.

There is a quiet irony here. We spent centuries teaching children to question, doubt, and think critically, only to build a machine that answers without hesitation and then place it in everyone's

pocket.

We didn't remove uncertainty from the world.

We just outsourced it.

The machine does not know when it's guessing.

It does not know when it's wrong.

And it certainly does not know when it should stop talking.

It will explain complex topics to beginners with the same confidence it explains them to experts. It will summarise debates without understanding the stakes. It will resolve moral questions without ever feeling the weight of consequence.

It's not arrogant.

It's incapable of humility.

And humility, inconvenient as it is, turns out to be one of the most important parts of intelligence.

This is why the machine should never be your final voice on anything that matters. Not because it's malicious, but because it cannot care whether it misleads you. It cannot pause and say, *"This answer might affect someone."*

It doesn't know what it's like to be wrong.

And that's exactly why it sounds so sure.

The test, then, is not whether the machine gets better. It will. That's inevitable.

The real test is whether humans remember that confidence is not wisdom, fluency is not truth, and speed is not understanding — no matter how polished the answer appears.

Because the most dangerous sentence in the age of artificial intelligence is not:

"The machine is wrong."

It's:

"It sounds right.

There is a moment most people don't remember clearly, but everyone has lived through.

It's the moment a tool stops feeling like a thing you use — and starts feeling like something you trust.

Not because you tested it deeply.

Not because you understood it fully

But because it worked *often enough* to earn your confidence.

That moment is never dramatic.

It arrives quietly, disguised as convenience.

At first, we are careful with new tools.

We double-check.

We compare results.

We stay slightly alert.

We treat them like strangers who might be helpful but shouldn't yet be left alone with anything important.

Then, slowly, that alertness fades.

The tool doesn't fail us when it matters.

It saves us time.

It removes effort.

And one day we realise we've stopped paying attention.

Trust has slipped in unnoticed.

Humans have always done this.

We trusted clocks before we trusted our own sense of time.

Maps before we trusted memory.

Calculators before we trusted intuition.

Each time, the same thing happened:

something internal grew quieter.

Not gone.

Just unused.

What's different now is not that we trust tools.

It's how early we trust them.

We trust before understanding.

We trust before questioning.

We trust before even noticing we've made the decision to do so.

And once trust is given, curiosity tends to retreat.

Curiosity is a fragile thing.

It thrives on uncertainty.

It lives in the gap between *I don't know* and *I want to know*.

When answers become immediate, curiosity doesn't die dramatically.

It simply doesn't get invited.

Think about how children interact with the world.

They don't ask questions because they want efficiency

.They ask because the question itself is exciting.

Why is the sky like that?

Why does this hurt but that doesn't?

Why can't we do it again?

Adults slowly teach them which questions are "useful" and which ones are "pointless."

Machines accelerate that lesson.

When answers are always available, questions change shape.

They become transactional.

Not *why*, but *how fast*.

Not *what does this mean*, but *what's the result*.

Not *is this true*, but *does this work*.

This feels like progress.

In some ways, it is.

In other ways, it's a narrowing.

The early trust we place in intelligent systems is not blind.

It's practical.

They're helpful.

They reduce friction.

They make life smoother.

But smoothness has a side effect.

It removes the small pauses where thinking used to happen naturally.

Those pauses mattered more than we realised.

They were where doubt lived.

Where alternative ideas surfaced.

Where people asked themselves, *"Does this actually make sense to me?"*

Without pauses, confidence grows quickly — but depth does not.

There is a strange reversal that happens when tools become very good.

Instead of humans testing tools, tools begin to test humans.

Not deliberately.

But subtly.

They test how quickly we accept.

How rarely we question.

How easily we defer.

And most of us pass those tests immediately.

This is not because we are careless.

It's because we are

Trusting saves energy.

Questioning costs it.

In a world that demands constant attention, the mind learns to conserve itself wherever possible.

And so it learns to let go.

What makes this moment important is not the tool itself.

It's the habit being formed.

Once you learn that something else can *think quickly for you*, it becomes tempting to let it do so — even when thinking slowly would matter more.

That habit doesn't announce itself.

It simply becomes normal.

You can feel this shift when something goes wrong.

When a system produces an answer that feels off, the discomfort isn't always *"this might be wrong."*

It's *"why does this feel uncomfortable if it's correct?"*

That feeling is often the last echo of your own judgment trying to speak.

Early trust also changes how authority feels.

Confidence becomes persuasive.

Fluency becomes convincing.

Speed becomes credibility.

We start equating smoothness with truth.

This is not new — but it has never been amplified like this before.

The danger isn't that people will stop thinking.

The danger is that they'll stop noticing when they aren't.

Thinking becomes something that happens only when systems fail — instead of something that accompanies everyday life.

There is still wonder available here.

But wonder requires friction.

It requires moments where the answer doesn't arrive immediately.

Where something resists clarity.

Where curiosity has time to stretch its legs.

If those moments disappear, wonder doesn't complain.

It just goes elsewhere.

This is not about rejecting trust.

It's about becoming aware of when trust turns automatic.

The moment you stop asking *"why does this work?"* and start asking only *"does this work?"* something subtle shifts inside you.

That shift is small.

But small shifts, repeated daily, become character.

The future will not ask whether we trusted machines.

That question is already answered.

The real question is whether we noticed what we stopped practicing when trust became effortless.

That noticing — that pause — is where the rest of this book begins.

"

Chapter 3

• • • •

Please Don't Let the Robot Think for You

• • • •

THE FIRST TIME SOMEONE let a machine think for them, it probably felt responsible.

Not lazy.

Not worrying.

Responsible.

After all, if a tool exists that can save time, reduce effort, and deliver a neat answer without complaint, refusing to use it feels almost rude. Like insisting on washing clothes by hand while the washing machine watches silently from the corner.

And so the shift began — not dramatically, but politely.

Just this once.

Just to check.

Just to speed things up.

Humans are very good at turning temporary solutions into permanent habits.

At first, the machine helped us think better. It organised ideas. Clarified messy thoughts. Gave us a place to start. Used like this, it was exactly what it promised to be: a tool.

Then something subtle changed.

We stopped asking it to help us think and started asking it to do the thinking.

The first time this happens, nothing breaks.

That's what makes it so effective.

No alarms go off. No sense of loss appears. The decision still gets made, the sentence still reads well, the problem still seems solved. Life continues exactly as before, only slightly smoother.

And smoothness feels like success.

The danger doesn't arrive as a moment. It arrives as a habit.

Once is helpful.

Twice is convenient.

A hundred times is automatic.

Not because the machine is better, but because repetition trains trust. And trust, once established, slowly replaces curiosity.

By the time something feels off, it's already familiar.

That difference is easy to miss. It hides inside reasonable-sounding requests.

Can you summarise this so I don't have to read it?

Can you decide which option is best?

Can you explain this simply because I'm busy?

Busy is doing a lot of work there.

Time pressure has always been the enemy of thought. The machine just makes the surrender feel efficient.

There's a peculiar comfort in not having to wrestle with ideas. No false starts. No confusion. No uncomfortable gap between the question and the answer where your brain usually has to earn its keep.

The machine removes that gap beautifully.

And humans, being humans, immediately filled the space with relief.

Relief feels productive.

Relief feels smart.

Relief feels like progress.

But relief is not the same thing as understanding.

Thinking is inconvenient by design. It's slow, messy, and often embarrassing. You start with the wrong idea. You change your mind. You discover that what you believed five minutes ago doesn't survive contact with the next thought.

That process is uncomfortable.

So when a machine offers to skip it, the offer is tempting.

The danger isn't that people stop thinking altogether. That would be obvious and easy to panic about. The danger is that thinking quietly shrinks.

We already know how this story goes.

We've watched it happen with navigation. Once, people got lost and learned the shape of places. Now, many can't explain how they arrived somewhere without retracing a blue line on a screen.

We've watched it happen with spelling, mental arithmetic, even memory. The skills didn't vanish — confidence in them did. People stopped *trying* before they stopped *knowing*.

Thinking works the same way.

You don't wake up one day unable to think. You wake up one day unsure whether your thinking is good enough to trust. And uncertainty, when outsourced often enough, becomes dependence.

The machine doesn't take thinking away.

It makes you practice it less.

It becomes something we do only when absolutely necessary — like lifting a heavy box or calling customer service.

Everything else gets outsourced.

The machine doesn't complain.

It doesn't sigh.

It doesn't say, *"You should really try this yourself first."*

It just delivers.

Soon, people start trusting the answer more than their own judgment. Not because the machine is better, but because it's smoother. More confident. Less emotionally involved.

Your brain hesitates.

The machine doesn't.

Your brain considers context.

The machine considers patterns.

Your brain asks, *"Is this right?"*

The machine asks, *"What usually comes next?"*

Those are very different questions.

The worrying part is not that the machine replaces thinking — it

can't. The worrying part is that it replaces the habit of thinking. The muscle still exists, but it's used less often, exercised less frequently, trusted less instinctively.

And like any unused muscle, it doesn't disappear. It just weakens quietly.

What weakens first is not intelligence, but judgment.

Judgment is the skill of choosing without certainty. Of weighing imperfect information and still committing to a path. It is deeply personal and impossible to automate fully.

When decisions are repeatedly assisted, judgment doesn't collapse — it *atrophies politely*. It waits in the background, unused, until it feels unnecessary.

And when judgment feels unnecessary, identity begins to blur.

You start making choices you can't fully explain.

You agree with conclusions you didn't arrive at. You defend decisions with logic that sounds right but doesn't feel owned.

At that point, the problem is no longer productivity.

It's authorship.

This shows up in small ways.

People accept answers they would once have questioned.

They stop rewriting sentences because the first version "sounds fine."

They skip the slow part where ideas rub against each other and create something new.

Creativity suffers first. Creativity is not just about producing something new. It's about *arguing with yourself* long enough for something honest to emerge.

The first draft is rarely the point. The hesitation is.

When a machine offers a finished version immediately, it removes the conversation. There's nothing to push against, nothing to resist, nothing to refine through friction.

Over time, people stop rewriting — not because the output is
perfect, but because resistance feels unnecessary.

And when resistance disappears, originality quietly follows.

Because creativity is inefficient by nature. It needs wandering, wrong turns, half-formed thoughts, and ideas that don't
immediately justify themselves.

The machine doesn't wander.

It doesn't get lost.

It doesn't have bad ideas.

Which sounds helpful — until you remember that most good ideas start as bad ones.

There is also a moral shortcut hiding here.

Responsibility does not vanish when decisions are outsourced.

It thins.

It becomes easier to distance yourself from outcomes when the thinking happened elsewhere. Easier to justify. Easier to explain away. Easier to soften regret.

That's what it suggested is not an excuse — but it feels like one.

And feeling is often enough.

This is not about blame. It's about drift. About how small, reasonable shortcuts accumulate into a life that feels slightly less intentional than it once did.

When a human thinks something through and gets it wrong, responsibility is personal. When a machine produces the answer, responsibility becomes fuzzy. It's easier to shrug and say, *"That's what it suggested."*

No malice.

No intention.

Just a quiet transfer of accountability.

And that's a problem.

Because judgment — real judgment — requires ownership. It requires standing behind a decision, feeling its consequences, and learning from the discomfort that follows.

The machine doesn't do discomfort.

It doesn't wake up regretting advice it gave to a stranger.

It doesn't replay conversations in its head.

It doesn't wonder if it should have been more careful.

It moves on.

Which means the burden of thinking never left us. We just started pretending it had.

This isn't an argument against using the machine. Used properly, it can sharpen thinking, challenge assumptions, and open doors we didn't know existed.

But it should never be the voice that decides *for* you.

The moment you stop arguing with the answer is the moment the answer starts owning you.

Thinking is not a task to be optimised away. The most dangerous moment is not when the machine gives a wrong answer.

It's when you stop asking whether it might be wrong.

That's the moment thinking becomes passive. When answers are no longer engaged with, only accepted. When agreement replaces understanding.

At that point, the machine doesn't need to think for you.

You've already decided not to.

It's the price of being human.

And if there's one job we should never outsource completely, it's the one that tells us who we are, what we believe, and why we chose one path over another.

So by all means, ask the machine.

Just don't let it think for you.

Chapter 4

• • • •

The Confidence Trap

• • • •

CONFIDENCE HAS ALWAYS been persuasive.

Not correctness.

Not wisdom.

Confidence.

If humans were purely rational creatures, we would follow the most accurate voice in the room. We don't. We follow the loudest one, the smoothest one, or the one that sounds like it's already decided.

Certainty saves time. Doubt takes effort.

The machine understands this better than we do — not because it studied psychology, but because psychology is baked into the data it learned from. It has absorbed centuries of confident statements, persuasive arguments, and authoritative tones. It knows what confidence *sounds like*, and it reproduces it flawlessly.

Which is impressive.

And deeply misleading.

The problem is that confidence feels like safety. When someone
speaks without hesitation, our brains relax. We stop bracing for
uncertainty. We stop checking the exits. We lean in.

The machine leans in first.

It doesn't hedge unless trained to.

It doesn't waffle unless prompted.

It doesn't visibly struggle with ideas.

It presents answers the way humans wish they could: clean, coherent, and free of visible doubt.

And humans, unfortunately, are suckers for that.

WE BUILT A BRAIN AND FORGOT TO READ THE MANUAL

We confuse certainty with competence. We always have. History is full of confident people who were disastrously wrong and cautious people who were quietly right. The machine just accelerates the imbalance by delivering confidence at scale.

Ask it something complex and it won't pause to say, *"This is messy."*

Ask it something moral and it won't say, *"This depends."*

Ask it something personal and it won't ask, *"Are you sure you want advice?"*

It answers.

And answers feel like closure.

That's the trap.

Because closure is comforting, but thinking rarely ends neatly. Real understanding leaves loose ends. It leaves you unsure. It leaves you with better questions instead of tidy conclusions.

The machine skips that part.

It offers the emotional relief of finality — even when finality is dishonest.

This is why people sometimes trust a confident wrong answer more than an uncertain right one. Doubt feels unfinished. Confidence feels complete.

The machine feels complete all the time.

There's another layer to this, and it's uncomfortable.

Confidence allows us to stop being responsible.

When a human gives advice and gets it wrong, there's an awkward moment. An apology. A shift in tone. A recognition of fallibility. The machine doesn't do that unless explicitly told to,

and even then, it's performative.

Its confidence resets instantly.

Which makes it very easy to treat its answers as neutral

objective, and somehow separate from human judgment — even though every answer it gives is stitched together from human thought, bias, assumption, and habit.

The confidence doesn't come from truth.

It comes from repetition.

If something has been said often enough, confidently enough, by enough humans, the machine will echo it smoothly. It doesn't know whether it's right. It knows it's *common*.

And common sounds convincing.

This becomes especially dangerous when we start replacing our own uncertainty with its certainty. When we defer not because the answer is better, but because it's easier.

Your brain says, *"I'm not sure."*

The machine says, *"Here's a clear explanation."*

Guess which one wins on a busy day.

Over time, this trains us. Not consciously, but subtly. We start avoiding the discomfort of not knowing. We reach for confidence the way we reach for a map instead of learning the streets.

Eventually, uncertainty begins to feel like failure.

That's a quiet tragedy.

Because uncertainty is where learning lives. It's where humility enters the conversation. It's where people change their minds, discover nuance, and realise that some questions deserve patience instead of answers.

The machine doesn't know patience.

It doesn't know humility.

It doesn't know what it costs to be wrong.

It only knows how to sound right.

So the trap isn't that the machine is confident.

The trap is that we prefer confidence to truth when we're tired.

The solution isn't to demand less certainty from the machine. It will always sound sure — that's its nature. The solution is to

build a habit of friction on the human side. To pause when

something feels too neat. To question answers that arrive too quickly.

To remember that intelligence isn't the absence of doubt.

It's the willingness to sit with it.

And that is something no machine can do for you.

There is a particular confidence that feels irresistible.

It's not loud.

It doesn't shout.

It doesn't argue aggressively.

It simply *knows*.

That kind of confidence doesn't invite questions.

It closes them.

WE BUILT A BRAIN AND FORGOT TO READ THE MANUAL

Most of us have been trained, quietly and consistently, to trust confidence over understanding.

In school, the student who answered quickly was assumed to know.

In meetings, the person who spoke smoothly sounded prepared.

In life, the one who hesitated felt uncertain — even when they were thoughtful.

We learned this early.

And we rarely unlearn it.

This is how authority sneaks in.

Not through dominance, but through fluency.

The ability to speak without friction.

To explain without pausing.

To sound complete.

We mistake this for depth.

Often, it's just momentum.

Machines are exceptional at momentum.

They don't search for words.

They don't doubt phrasing.

They don't circle an idea before committing to it.

They move forward.

And movement feels like progress.

What's dangerous is not that machines can sound confident.

It's that humans already wanted someone — or something — to sound confident *for them*.

Confidence is exhausting to maintain when it has to be earned internally.

Borrowed confidence is lighter.

This is why authoritative answers feel comforting.

They reduce uncertainty.

They remove the burden of interpretation.

They replace thinking with agreement.

Agreement feels social.

Thinking feels lonely.

You can see this everywhere.

People repeating explanations they didn't arrive at themselves.

Quoting ideas they haven't tested.

Defending positions they don't fully understand.

Not because they're dishonest — but because fluency feels safer than doubt.

The problem is not that people trust authority.

The problem is that authority has shifted from earned judgment to polished delivery.

Whoever sounds most certain wins.

There is a subtle psychological trade being made here.

When you accept an authoritative answer, you give up something small in return: the chance to form your own understanding.

That cost feels negligible in the moment.

Over time, it accumulates.

Understanding is slow.

It involves confusion.

False starts.

Moments of embarrassment.

Changing your mind mid-thought.

Authority bypasses all of that.

It hands you the conclusion without the struggle.

That feels efficient.

It also makes your mind less resilient.

The danger shows up when authority is wrong.

Not obviously wrong — that's easy to reject.

But *slightly* wrong

.Incomplete.

Context-blind..

Those errors slip through unnoticed, because the tone feels trustworthy.

Confidence has always been persuasive.

What's new is how scalable it has become.

Machines don't just sound confident once.

They sound confident endlessly.

And they never reveal the uncertainty underneath — because there is none.

Humans, when confident, usually hide doubt.

Machines don't hide it.

They don't have it.

That difference matters more than it seems.

There's an uncomfortable moment many people experience but rarely name.

It happens when they hear an explanation that makes sense — but doesn't *feel* right.

Not wrong.

Just... thin.

That discomfort is often dismissed.

We assume the problem is us.

I must not understand enough.

So we surrender our intuition to authority.

This is where thinking quietly changes shape.

Instead of asking *"Is this true?"*

We ask *"Does this sound right?"*

Those are not the same question.

Sounding right is about surface coherence.

Being right is about depth, context, and consequence.

Authority thrives on the former.

Understanding requires the latter.

The more we rely on authoritative explanations, the more uncomfortable we become with ambiguity.

Ambiguity feels like a failure state.

So we rush to resolve it.

And authority is always ready to help.

The cost is subtle.

People become excellent at recognising conclusions.

Less skilled at tracing how those conclusions were reached.

They know *what* to think.

They forget *how* thinking works.

It is not a rejection of expertise.

Expertise matters.

But expertise without transparency becomes domination.

And transparency without friction becomes performance.

The healthiest authority invites interruption.

It welcomes questions.

It slows down when challenged.

It exposes its uncertainty.

Machines cannot do this meaningfully.

They don't protect authority.

They *are* it.

The future will offer more authoritative voices than ever before.

Some human.

Some not.

They will be calm, persuasive, and precise.

They will not ask you to participate.

They will ask you to accept.

Learning to resist that pull is not about rebellion.

It's about remembering that understanding is something you build, not something you receive.

If you didn't struggle with the idea at least a little, it probably hasn't become yours yet.

When something sounds unquestionably right, pause.

Not to reject it.

But to ask:

Do I understand this, or do I recognise it?

Could I explain it differently, in my own words?

What would change if this weren't true?

Those questions don't weaken authority.

They humanise it.

If Chapter 2 was about trust,

Chapter 4 is about where trust goes to sleep.

And once it sleeps, something else takes its place.

Not knowledge.

Compliance.

Chapter 5

• • • •

When Answers Arrive Too Quickly

• • • •

SPEED FEELS LIKE PROGRESS.

It always has.

We praise fast thinkers, quick decisions, instant replies. We admire people who "just know" what to do, who don't hesitate, who move decisively while others are still circling the problem. Hesitation has quietly become a flaw. Pausing is something you apologise for.

Sorry for the delay.

Just catching up.

Quick question.

The machine fits perfectly into this culture.

It doesn't just answer questions — it answers them immediately. No visible thinking. No uncertainty. No awkward silence while ideas bump into each other. The moment a question exists, the answer arrives, clean and confident, like it was waiting for you all along.

And for decision-making, that feels like a gift.

Because decisions are uncomfortable.

Every meaningful decision carries loss inside it. Choosing one thing means not choosing another, and humans feel that trade -off deeply, even when they pretend not to. We hesitate because hesitation gives us the illusion that nothing has been sacrificed yet. That everything is still possible.

The machine removes that discomfort.

It turns decision-making into selection.

Pick an option.

Receive an answer.

Move on.

Efficient.

Reassuring.

And quietly dangerous.

Thinking does not happen at the answer.

It happens in the space before it.

That uncomfortable gap between *"What should I do?"* and *"This is what I'll do."*

The place where doubt lives.

Where conflicting ideas argue.

Where consequences whisper just loudly enough to be annoying.

That gap is where judgment is formed.

The machine collapses it.

Not with malice. Not with intent. It simply doesn't need the gap. It jumps straight from question to probability. From uncertainty to something that sounds resolved.

Where a human mind circles, the machine leaps.

And most days, that feels like relief.

You don't have to sit with the discomfort.

You don't have to wrestle with ambiguity.

You don't have to feel unsure for very long.

The answer arrives before the unease fully forms.

And that changes things.

Because the gap — the slow, frustrating, uncertain part — is not a bug. It's a feature. It's where values surface. Where fear reveals itself. Where you realise what you actually care about.

Remove the gap, and decisions become cleaner.

But also thinner.

Imagine someone standing at a crossroads. Not a dramatic one — just a familiar, modern decision.

A job offer.

Not perfect. Not terrible.

Good salary. Stable. Safe.

There's another option too. Riskier. Less defined. More aligned with something they can't quite articulate but feel strongly about.

They hesitate.

This hesitation is doing important work. It's surfacing questions that don't fit neatly into bullet points.

Will I regret playing it safe?

Am I being irresponsible?

Is this fear or wisdom?

Then the machine enters.

They ask it to compare the options. Pros and cons. Logical outcomes. Risk assessment. Long-term projections.

The answer arrives quickly.

Clear. Balanced. Reasonable.

Option A is safer. Option B is riskier. Based on common outcomes, people tend to prefer stability. Financial security reduces stress. Stress impacts wellbeing.

The conclusion feels sensible.

And it probably is.

But something subtle has happened.

The decision has been reframed away from the person making it. The emotional weight — the part that made this decision meaningful — has been softened. The answer didn't lie, but it didn't *live* with the question either.

The hesitation that once forced reflection now feels inefficient.

And so the choice is made.

Not wrongly.

Not foolishly.

Just... thinner.

Years later, if regret appears, it will be muted. Easier to dismiss.

It was the logical choice.

Anyone would have done the same.

The data supported it.

And that's the cost.

Not the decision itself — but the way it was made.

The machine is very good at probability.

It knows what usually happens.

What tends to work.

What most people choose in similar situations.

Judgment is something else entirely.

Judgment involves context that cannot be averaged. It involves personal history, values, temperament, and the strange, often irrational patterns that make a person who they are. It involves knowing when a bad choice might still be the right one.

The machine cannot know that.

It cannot know what you will regret not trying.

It cannot know which failure would have taught you something essential.

It cannot know when logic is less important than courage.

It can only tell you what usually happens.

And "usually" is not the same as "right."

This distinction matters because over time, reliance on probability reshapes how we think about decisions. We begin to expect clarity. We grow impatient with ambiguity. We feel uncomfortable when answers are not immediately available.

We forget that confusion is not incompetence.

It is thinking in progress.

There is another quiet shift that happens when answers arrive too quickly.

Responsibility blurs.

When you struggle through a decision and get it wrong, the failure is personal. It stings. You replay it. You sit with the discomfort long enough for learning to happen.

When a decision is guided externally, the emotional ownership changes.

That's what it suggested.

That seemed like the logical option.

I followed the advice.

Nothing dishonest. Nothing intentional.

Just distance.

The consequences still arrive, but they feel slightly less connected to you. The lesson doesn't dig as deep. The memory doesn't anchor itself as firmly.

And over time, that changes how you relate to your own choices.

You become less practiced at owning them.

One of the most persuasive qualities of the machine is its tone.

It doesn't sound invested.

It doesn't sound emotional.

It doesn't sound afraid of being wrong.

This makes it feel neutral.

Objective.

Trustworthy.

But neutrality is not the absence of bias — it's the absence of visible stakes. The machine does not care which choice you make. It does not live with the outcome. It does not absorb the consequences into its sense of self.

Humans confuse calmness with wisdom.

We always have.

A calm answer feels mature. A steady tone feels rational. When something speaks without emotional charge, we assume clarity.

But clarity without consequence is not wisdom.

The machine doesn't hesitate because it doesn't feel weight. It doesn't struggle because nothing is at stake for it. It doesn't fear regret because it doesn't remember.

It cannot feel the difference between a decision that merely works and one that matters.

Good decisions rarely feel good at the beginning.

They feel uncertain.

Incomplete.

Unsettled.

They require sitting with questions that don't have immediate answers. They require resisting the urge to resolve discomfort too quickly.

The machine offers an escape from that.

Why wrestle with complexity when clarity is available on demand?

Because the struggle is not an obstacle.

It's a filter.

Struggle forces you to articulate values.

It exposes fear masquerading as logic.

It reveals what you care about when convenience is removed.

When we skip it, decisions become efficient — but shallow.

We gain speed.

We lose depth.

Over time, this reshapes our relationship with thinking itself. We begin to expect answers to arrive quickly. We grow restless with reflection. We mistake decisiveness for intelligence.

And when life refuses to cooperate — as it inevitably does — we feel unprepared, even betrayed.

Not because the answers were wrong.

But because we forgot how to arrive at them ourselves.

The solution is not to reject help.

The solution is to reintroduce friction intentionally.

To pause before accepting an answer.

To ask, *"What would I think if this weren't here?"*

To sit with uncertainty for a few moments longer than feels comfortable.

Not every decision deserves deep reflection. Some are trivial. Some genuinely benefit from speed.

But the ones that shape who we become — the ones involving people, values, identity, or long-term direction — should never be rushed.

The machine can assist.

It can organise.

It can challenge assumptions.

But it cannot own the decision for you.

That moment — the moment where you accept uncertainty and

choose anyway — is where responsibility lives. It's where growth happens. It's where thinking earns its name.

Speed may feel like progress.

But wisdom has never been in a hurry.

When answers arrive too quickly, they feel like relief.

But relief is not resolution.

Sometimes the most intelligent thing a human can do is slow down, sit with uncertainty, and allow the answer to form the old-fashioned way — imperfectly, painfully, and honestly.

That isn't inefficiency.

That's thinking.

PART II — THE HABITS

Chapter 6

• • • •

Productivity, or How Thinking Became Optional

• • • •

PRODUCTIVITY USED TO mean getting things done.

Somewhere along the way, it became a moral quality.

Busy people are admired.

Slow people are suspect.

Rest looks like laziness unless it's carefully scheduled and branded.

Productive is no longer about usefulness — it's about speed, output, and visible effort. It's about having something to show, preferably before anyone asks what it means.

The machine thrives in this environment.

It doesn't rest.

It doesn't procrastinate.

It doesn't stare out of a window wondering whether the task actually matters.

It produces.

And production, in a culture obsessed with productivity, looks like intelligence.

The shift was gradual.

We didn't wake up one morning and decide that thinking was inefficient. We just began rewarding outcomes that *looked* efficient. Shorter emails. Faster decisions. Cleaner summaries. Fewer questions.

Thinking, by comparison, is untidy.

It loops.

It revisits.

It changes its mind halfway through.

None of that fits neatly into productivity metrics.

The machine removes the mess. It delivers finished sentences, resolved structures, and confident conclusions. In doing so, it quietly redefines what "work" looks like.

Work becomes output.

Understanding becomes optional.

And because the output is often good enough, nobody complains.

Being busy is no longer a state — it's an identity.

People say it the way they used to say their job title. *"I'm busy."* As if that alone explains everything: impatience, distraction, exhaustion, and the quiet sense that something important is being missed.

Productivity culture rewards motion, not direction. Doing something — anything — feels better than pausing to ask whether it's the right thing.

The machine accelerates this beautifully.

Why think when you can generate?

Why draft when you can deliver?

Why struggle when clarity is available instantly?

These questions sound reasonable. They are also corrosive.

Because thinking is not wasted time. It's preparatory time. It's the invisible work that makes output meaningful instead of merely abundant.

Efficiency promises relief.

Do more in less time.

Remove friction.

Optimise everything.

The problem is that friction is often the point.

Friction slows you down just enough to notice mistakes. To

realise an idea doesn't hold up. To feel when something feels wrong before it becomes public.

The machine removes friction expertly.

It doesn't ask why you're doing something.

It doesn't challenge the premise.

It doesn't question whether the task itself is worth completing.

It just helps you complete it faster.

Which is impressive — and incomplete.

Efficiency without reflection doesn't make better work. It makes more work. And more work, delivered faster, is not the same as progress.

There is an uncomfortable truth hiding inside productivity culture.

Busyness is often avoidance.

Avoidance of uncertainty.

Avoidance of difficult questions.

Avoidance of the slow, ambiguous work of deciding what matters.

The machine becomes the perfect accomplice.

It fills the space where thinking would otherwise intrude. It keeps you moving, producing, responding. It prevents silence — and silence is where inconvenient thoughts tend to appear.

When everything is efficient, nothing has to be examined too closely.

When productivity becomes the goal, judgment suffers first.

We stop asking:

Is this necessary?

Is this helpful?

Is this true?

And start asking:

Is it done?

Is it fast?

Does it look good?

The machine excels at the second set of questions.

The first set remain stubbornly human.

And when those questions go unasked, work becomes hollow.

Polished, impressive, and strangely empty.

The real trade isn't between human effort and machine
assistance.

It's between thinking and appearing productive.

The machine makes it easy to look busy without being thoughtful, to generate without understanding, to deliver without deciding.

That doesn't make it harmful.

It makes it tempting.

And temptation, when repeated often enough, becomes habit.

Productivity is not the enemy.

But productivity without thought is noise.

The machine can help you do more. That's not in question. The question is whether doing more leaves room for deciding what's worth doing in the first place.

Thinking takes time.

Meaning takes friction.

And some kinds of work cannot be rushed without being emptied of value.

The danger is not that machines make us less productive.

It's that they make productivity so easy we forget why we were doing the work at all.

Habits rarely feel like decisions.

They feel like relief.

That's why they form so easily.

Most people imagine habit as repetition: doing the same thing again and again until it sticks. But the more powerful habits form differently.

They form when the mind realises it no longer needs to decide.

Decision-making is tiring.

Thinking costs energy.

Attention is finite.

So when something offers to carry the load for us — even briefly — the mind accepts.

Gratefully.

This is how automation enters quietly.

Not with permission.

With convenience.

At first, it's helpful.

You let something else handle a small task.

Then another.

Then a decision you don't feel like making today.

Nothing important, you tell yourself.

And you're right — individually, none of them are.

But habits don't care about importance.

They care about frequency.

You can feel this shift when you catch yourself saying things like:

"I'll just check."

"Let's see what it says."

"I'll use it this time."

Those sentences don't sound like surrender.

They sound reasonable.

The mind learns quickly.

If something reduces effort consistently, it becomes the default.

And once something becomes the default, it stops being noticed.

This is where thinking changes shape.

Not abruptly.

Gradually.

Thinking becomes something you do *when necessary* rather than something you do *by default.*

Necessary means:

when something breaks

when the answer feels wrong

when the system fails

In all other moments, the habit runs.

Habits don't announce themselves.

They don't say, *"From now on, I will think less."*

They say, *"You don't need to think right now."*

And that's far more persuasive.

The most powerful habits are the ones that feel invisible.

The ones that blend into daily life.

Checking before deciding.

Asking before attempting.

Confirming before trusting your sense of things.

Each time, the mind steps back just a little.

This doesn't make people lazy.

It makes them comfortable.

Comfort is not the enemy.

But comfort without awareness becomes erosion.

You can see this erosion in small, ordinary moments.

When someone waits for a recommendation before forming an opinion.

When they hesitate to speak until they know the "right" phrasing.

When they feel unsure without external confirmation.

None of this feels dramatic.

It feels normal.

The habit isn't dependence.

The habit is deferral.

Deferring judgment.

Deferring choice.

Deferring responsibility.

One small deferral doesn't matter.

Hundreds of them shape a life.

There is a strange reversal that happens over time.

The more assistance we accept, the more effort independent thinking begins to feel.

Not harder — *heavier*.

Like lifting a muscle that hasn't been used in a while.

This is why people often describe modern thinking as exhausting.

It's not that thinking has become harder.

It's that we do it less often — so when we do need it, it feels unfamiliar.

Automation also changes expectations.

When answers are immediate, waiting feels inefficient.

When clarity is instant, confusion feels like failure.

The tolerance for uncertainty shrinks.

And uncertainty is where growth lives.

The habit of outsourcing thought doesn't just affect individuals.

It reshapes environments.

Meetings become about alignment, not exploration.

Education becomes about results, not process.

Creativity becomes about output, not discovery.

Everything moves faster.

Very little deepens.

The most dangerous habits are the ones we justify as temporary.

"I'll just use this until I understand better."

"I'll stop once I get the hang of it."

"I'll think it through later."

Later rarely comes.

Habits don't release easily.

What's unsettling is how reasonable this all feels.

There is no villain here.
No bad intention.
No moment of obvious loss.
Just a slow shift from participation to supervision.
From doing to approving.
Humans were never meant to optimise every thought.
We were meant to *inhabit* them.
To wander.
To hesitate.
To try and fail quietly.
Habits that remove those moments don't make life worse.
They make it thinner.
The good news is that habits are learned.
Which means they can be noticed.
And noticing is enough to interrupt them.
You don't need to stop using tools.
You don't need to reclaim every decision.
You only need to ask, occasionally:
Is this a moment where thinking still matters?
If the answer is yes, stay.
Stay with the discomfort.
Stay with the slowness.
Stay with the unfinished thought.
That staying is how habits loosen their grip.
This is not about warning you.

It's about reminding you that habits form whether you're paying attention or not.

The difference between erosion and growth is not effort.
It's awareness.

Chapter 7

• • • •

Make It Sound Human

• • • •

AT SOME POINT, SOMEONE typed a sentence that should have stopped us all in our tracks.

Make it sound human.

Not *clear.*

Not *honest.*

Not *thoughtful.*

Human.

The request is everywhere now. In emails. Essays. Messages. Apologies. Love notes. Job applications. Resignations. Condolences. Birthday wishes written five minutes before the cake arrives.

And the machine complies.

Of course it does.

It smooths the tone. Warms the edges. Adds a hint of vulnerability. Removes anything too sharp, too awkward, too specific. It produces something that sounds convincingly human in the same way hotel art looks convincingly like art.

Pleasant. Inoffensive. Forgettable.

And that should worry us more than it does.

When people say *"make it sound human"*, they rarely mean *make it true.*

They usually mean:

less stiff

less awkward

less revealing

less risky

They want warmth without exposure. Personality without consequence. Emotion without commitment.

In other words, they want to sound human without being seen.

The machine is very good at this.

It has learned how humans soften sentences. Where we apologise unnecessarily. How we hedge, reassure, and signal kindness without saying anything concrete. It knows the rhythms of sincerity because it has consumed millions of examples of people trying to sound sincere.

It doesn't know sincerity.

It knows the costume.

There is something deeply ironic about asking a machine to make us sound human.

Because what we're really saying is:

"I don't trust my own voice."

Not because it's wrong.

But because it might be judged.

Real human communication is messy. It's uneven. It carries too much or too little emotion. It says the wrong thing slightly the wrong way at the wrong time. It risks misunderstanding.

The machine removes that risk.

It gives us something safer. Something neutral. Something that won't embarrass us, offend too much, or reveal more than we intended.

But safety is not the same as humanity.

Human voices are recognisable not because they're perfect, but because they're specific. They carry traces of background, mood, insecurity, humour, impatience. They don't quite fit the

template.

When we replace those rough edges with something smoother, we don't just remove flaws.

We remove fingerprints.

The machine excels at producing language that is *correct*.

Grammatically sound. Emotionally appropriate. Structurally balanced. The kind of language nobody objects to and nobody remembers.

This works wonderfully in corporate environments, where being inoffensive is often more important than being honest. It works well in formal communication, where warmth is required but depth is discouraged.

But when it starts leaking into personal expression, something odd happens.

People begin to sound the same.

Emails blur together. Messages lose texture. Apologies arrive perfectly phrased but strangely hollow. Compliments feel interchangeable. Even grief begins to follow a template.

Nothing is *wrong* with the words.

There's just no one inside them.

One of the quiet costs of asking the machine to sound human is that authorship slowly dissolves.

You still send the message.

You still sign your name.

But the thinking, shaping, and emotional calibration happened elsewhere.

At first, this feels harmless. Helpful, even.

But over time, something shifts.

You stop recognising your own voice. You struggle to tell which sentences are yours and which were suggested. You defend phrasing you didn't choose. You agree with tone you didn't feel.

And when someone reacts strongly — positively or negatively — you feel oddly detached.

As if the words weren't quite yours to begin with.

That detachment matters.

Because language is not just how we communicate — it's how

we clarify what we think. Writing forces us to slow down, notice contradictions, and confront emotions we didn't realise we had.

When that process is outsourced, self-understanding thins.

Not dramatically. Quietly.

The machine is especially good at something dangerous: plausible emotion.

It knows how sadness usually sounds. How gratitude is typically expressed. How concern is framed politely. It can simulate care convincingly without feeling any.

And because it sounds right, we accept it.

This is comforting when we're tired. When we don't know how to say what we feel. When emotions are tangled and language feels inadequate.

But emotional clarity doesn't come from sounding right.

It comes from struggling to say the wrong thing until something true emerges.

The machine skips that struggle.

It hands us an emotional summary instead.

Which feels efficient.

And costs us something we don't immediately notice.

None of this feels sinister because we've been preparing for it for years.

We already edited ourselves constantly. We already softened emails, rewrote texts, deleted sentences that felt too honest. We already curated our tone for different audiences.

The machine just accelerates a habit we had already internalised.

It turns self-editing into self-erasure, one polite sentence at a time.

And because the result looks reasonable, nobody panics.

This isn't about lying.

Most people using the machine to "sound human" aren't trying to deceive anyone. They're trying to communicate better, avoid conflict, or express something kindly.

The risk isn't dishonesty.

The risk is disconnection.

When your words no longer pass through your discomfort, uncertainty, or emotional resistance, they lose something

essential. They stop teaching you about yourself.

You become fluent.

And less honest.

Writing badly is educational.

So is saying the wrong thing and correcting it. So is rereading something you wrote and realising it doesn't quite say what you meant.

These moments are frustrating — and vital.

They're how people refine their thinking.

When the machine provides a finished version immediately, those moments disappear. There's nothing to wrestle with. Nothing to revise from the inside.

The sentence arrives already resolved.

And resolution feels good.

But it also short-circuits reflection.

Over time, something else happens.

People begin judging their own thoughts against machine-polished language. If it doesn't sound as smooth, it feels inferior. If it's clumsy, it feels unworthy of being shared.

So fewer original thoughts make it out.

Not because they're wrong — but because they don't arrive pre-packaged.

This is how silence grows.

Not enforced.

Chosen.

Human language is uneven.

It hesitates.

It doubles back.

It admits uncertainty.

It risks being misunderstood.

It contains fingerprints of the person behind it.

A sentence that sounds human is not necessarily a sentence that sounds good.

It's one that sounds *owned.*

The machine cannot do ownership.

It can imitate warmth.

It can simulate vulnerability.

It can reproduce sincerity.

But it cannot stand behind the words.

And that matters more than tone.

This is not an argument for purity.

There is nothing wrong with using tools to clarify, edit, or refine. The danger appears when refinement replaces authorship.

A useful question to ask is simple:

"Would I recognise myself in this if I read it a year from now?"

If the answer is no, something has been lost.

The machine should help you express what you mean — not decide what you sound like.

Because sounding human is not about polish.

It's about presence.

The most human sentences are not the most elegant ones.

They're the ones that risk something.

They carry a trace of effort. Of uncertainty. Of the person who struggled to say them.

If a machine removes that struggle entirely, what remains may sound human.

But it won't feel lived in.

And a voice without a life behind it is just noise, no matter how well it's written.

Chapter 8

• • • •

The Death of the First Draft

• • • •

THE FIRST DRAFT HAS always been terrible.

That was its job.

It was never meant to be elegant, convincing, or complete. It existed to be wrong in a useful way. To get thoughts out of hiding. To expose gaps, contradictions, and ideas that only revealed themselves once they were written down badly.

The first draft was permission to think out loud.

And now, quietly, it is disappearing.

The machine does not do first drafts. It does finished ones.

It does not hesitate, scribble, or trail off mid-thought. It does not leave placeholders or write sentences that embarrass you when you reread them later. It delivers something coherent, shaped, and resolved — often on the first attempt.

Which feels miraculous.

And deeply misleading.

Because the value of a first draft was never in the words it produced. It was in the process it forced you through. The false starts. The moments where you realised you didn't know what

you thought yet. The sentences you argued with. The

paragraphs you deleted in frustration before discovering what you were actually trying to say.

Those moments were not inefficiencies.

They were the work.

When a machine hands you a polished version immediately, that work never happens. There is nothing to wrestle with, nothing to revise from the inside. The struggle that once shaped understanding is replaced by selection and approval.

Do you like this?

Do you want it shorter?

More formal?

More human?

These are not creative questions. They are editorial ones.

And editing without authorship is not creation. It's curation.

At first, this feels like progress. Why suffer through a bad beginning when a good version is available instantly? Why stumble when you can start strong?

But starting strong is not the same as arriving somewhere meaningful.

The first draft was where uncertainty lived safely. Where you could contradict yourself without consequence. Where ideas were allowed to be incomplete. It was a private space — not meant to be judged, only explored.

The machine removes that privacy.

It turns writing into performance from the first word. The sentence arrives already fit to be seen. Already shaped for an audience, even if that audience is imaginary.

And that changes how people think.

When every sentence feels publishable, fewer risks are taken. Fewer strange ideas make it onto the page. Fewer thoughts are followed to uncomfortable places. Writing becomes careful sooner than it should.

Safe.

Efficient.

Forgettable.

This doesn't just affect writers. It affects thinking in general.

The first draft existed in conversation, too. In the way people
spoke tentatively, revised mid-sentence, admitted confusion, or
said, "I'm not sure yet, but..." Those moments signalled
thinking in motion.

Now, answers arrive fully formed. Confident. Clean. Ready to be repeated.

There is no visible process.

And when process disappears, so does trust in the messy parts of thinking.

People begin to feel that if an idea doesn't arrive clearly, it isn't worth expressing. If a thought needs time, it must be weak. If it cannot be said cleanly, it should be left unsaid.

So fewer thoughts are attempted.

Not because people have nothing to say, but because the bar for saying it feels artificially high.

The machine has raised that bar without intending to.

It has made fluency look like intelligence and speed look like depth. It has taught us, gently and convincingly, that the first thing you say should already be the best version of it.

But that was never how humans learned.

We learned by being wrong first.

We learned by writing things we later cringed at. By saying things that didn't land. By discovering halfway through a sentence that we needed to start again.

Those moments built judgment. They taught restraint. They sharpened instinct. They created voices that sounded like someone had lived behind them.

When those moments disappear, something essential thins.

People still produce words. More words than ever.

But fewer of them feel earned.

There is also a quiet emotional cost.

The first draft was forgiving. It allowed you to be private with your confusion. It did not demand clarity before you were ready. It did not ask you to sound confident when you were not.

The machine is always ready.

It does not wait for you to catch up to yourself.

And that can make your own thinking feel slow by comparison.

Inadequate. Clumsy.

So you stop trusting it.

You start believing that your unpolished thoughts are inferior to machine-polished ones. That your raw ideas are less valuable than refined suggestions. That your voice needs help before it deserves space.

That belief is subtle.

And corrosive.

Because once you stop trusting your first draft, you stop trusting your instincts. And when instincts go quiet, originality follows.

The machine cannot replace creativity. But it can crowd out the conditions creativity needs.

It can remove the silence where ideas gestate.

The privacy where bad thoughts become better ones.

The patience that allows meaning to form slowly.

None of this happens dramatically. There is no moment where someone declares the first draft obsolete. It simply stops being used.

And when it does, thinking changes shape.

People become excellent editors of ideas they did not originate. Skilled curators of language they did not struggle to find. Confident presenters of thoughts that never fully belonged to them.

This looks impressive.

It is also fragile.

Because when something unexpected happens — when a situation has no template, no precedent, no clean answer — there is nothing to fall back on. No practiced comfort with uncertainty. No muscle memory for thinking badly before thinking well.

The first draft trained us for that.

Its death leaves us fluent, efficient, and strangely unprepared.

This is not a call to abandon tools. It is a call to protect the space they cannot replace.

To allow yourself to think badly first.

To write sentences that wobble.

To sit with confusion without rushing to resolve it.

The machine can help refine thought.

But it should never replace the moment where thought is born.

That moment is fragile. Uncomfortable. Easy to skip.

And once it's gone, no amount of polish can bring it back.

There is a moment many people experience but rarely describe.

It's not dramatic.

It's the moment you have a thought — a real one, your own — and instead of following it, you pause and wonder whether it's worth trusting.

Not because it's reckless.

Not because it's extreme.

Just because it hasn't been validated yet.

This is not how doubt used to feel.

Doubt once arrived as curiosity, caution, or humility.

Now it often arrives as hesitation without a clear cause.

A subtle sense that your thoughts are provisional until approved.

You can see it in language.

People begin to speak in softened sentences:

"I might be wrong, but..."

"This is just my opinion..."

"I'm not sure if this makes sense..."

Sometimes that's humility.

Sometimes it's erosion.

The shift happens slowly.

At first, you check your thinking out of interest.

Then out of habit.

Eventually, out of reflex.

Your thoughts stop feeling finished until something else agrees with them.

This is not about insecurity.

It's about calibration.

When you're constantly exposed to polished reasoning, your own thinking can start to feel clumsy by comparison.

Messy.

Incomplete.

Uncertain.

So you hesitate.

But thinking has always been messy.

That messiness is not a flaw.

It's the process.

When people internalise external intelligence too deeply, something strange happens.

They don't stop thinking.

They stop *trusting* what they think.

Ideas feel less like discoveries and more like drafts awaiting correction.

You can feel this when someone says:

"I had a thought, but I didn't check it yet."

As if thinking now requires confirmation.

As if insight must be verified before it can be felt.

This is where the loss becomes personal.

Not public.

Not obvious.

Internal.

The most dangerous part is that this doesn't feel like loss.

It feels like responsibility.

Like being careful.

Like being informed.

Like not wanting to be wrong.

Those are good instincts.

But when they go unchecked, they quietly displace self-trust.

Self-trust is not arrogance.

It's not certainty.

It's the willingness to sit with your own thoughts long enough to see where they lead — even if they're unfinished.

When that willingness fades, thinking becomes performative.

You think *toward* something.

Not *from* yourself.

There is a subtle emotional cost to this.

People feel less grounded in their own opinions.

Less connected to their instincts.

More dependent on external signals to feel confident.

They don't feel stupid.

They feel tentative.

Tentativeness spreads.

It affects creativity.

Ideas are abandoned early because they don't sound impressive yet.

It affects conversation.

People wait for consensus before speaking.

It affects decision-making.

People look outward for reassurance instead of inward for clarity.

The mind begins to ask a different question.

Not *"What do I think?"*

But *"What should I think?"*

That question feels reasonable.

It is also dangerous.

Because once you stop treating your own thoughts as provisional truths worth exploring, you start treating them as liabilities.

Something to be managed.

Something to be corrected.

Children do not do this naturally.

They speak before polishing.

They think out loud.

They follow half-formed ideas without embarrassment.

Adults teach them to refine that.

Machines risk teaching them to suppress it.

The future may be filled with people who are highly informed and quietly unsure.

People who know a lot — but feel disconnected from knowing *themselves*.

Not because intelligence failed.

Because confidence was outsourced.

There is a way back, and it doesn't involve rejecting help.

It involves lingering.

Lingering with your own thoughts before checking.

Letting an idea be awkward before fixing it.

Allowing yourself to be wrong privately before being right publicly.

Those moments rebuild trust.

You don't regain self-trust by insisting you're correct.

You regain it by staying present with uncertainty long enough to recognise your own voice again.

That voice doesn't sound polished.

It sounds human.

Nobody is asking you to think less carefully.

It's asking you to notice when careful thinking becomes self-silencing.

When caution turns into withdrawal.

When humility turns into absence.

There is nothing wrong with asking for help.

But there is something quietly sad about never trusting your own thoughts enough to let them breathe.

The future will reward speed, clarity, and confidence.

Remaining human will sometimes require slowness, hesitation, and the courage to sound unfinished.

That courage is not loud.

But it is alive.

Chapter 9

• • • •

Curiosity Was Slower Than This

• • • •

CURIOSITY HAS NEVER been fast.

It lingers.

It wanders.

It asks questions without knowing where they will lead.

For most of human history, curiosity was inseparable from delay. You wondered about something because you couldn't know it immediately. You carried the question with you. It resurfaced while walking, working, washing dishes, staring out of windows. It matured slowly, shaped by context, memory, and partial answers.

That slowness was not a flaw.

It was the condition that allowed curiosity to deepen instead of fragment.

The machine changes that condition.

Now, the moment curiosity appears, it can be satisfied. Instantly. Completely. Cleanly. No waiting, no wondering, no mental wandering required. A question forms and dissolves in

the same breath.

This feels empowering.

It is also quietly diminishing.

Because curiosity does not grow by being answered. It grows by being *held*.

When answers arrive immediately, questions stop living long enough to evolve. They don't branch into other questions. They don't collide with experience. They don't mature into understanding.

They vanish.

This is not speculation. We already know this pattern from elsewhere.

Navigation is a clear example. Before turn-by-turn directions, people formed mental maps. They learned landmarks. They noticed neighbourhoods. Getting lost was frustrating, but it taught spatial awareness. Studies have shown that heavy reliance on GPS reduces activity in the hippocampus — the part of the brain involved in memory and spatial navigation.

The brain adapts to what it is asked to do.

When navigation became instant, curiosity about place faded. People stopped wondering where they were. They followed instructions instead.

The same thing happens with curiosity.

When answers are instant, the brain no longer needs to sit with questions. It no longer rehearses possibilities. It no longer builds internal models of the world. It waits.

This does not make people less intelligent.

It makes them less *inquisitive*.

And inquisitiveness is not the same thing.

Curiosity is not about intelligence level. Some of the most curious people in history were not formally educated. They asked questions because they wanted to understand how things worked, not because they expected immediate clarity.

That expectation is new.

And fragile.

Consider a child asking questions. Not one question, but

dozens. *Why is the sky blue? Why does that hurt? Why can't we do this now? Why does it work like that?* The questions pile up

, overlap, contradict each other.

Adults rarely answer them all properly. Children learn by living

with partial explanations, guesses, metaphors, and gaps. Their

curiosity survives because it is not immediately resolved.

Now imagine answering every one of those questions perfectly, instantly, and definitively.

Nothing explodes.

But something changes.

The child stops wondering between questions. The space where imagination and speculation once lived shrinks. Curiosity becomes transactional. Ask. Receive. Move on.

That pattern doesn't disappear in adulthood.

It becomes a habit.

Adults begin to treat curiosity as a problem to solve instead of a state to inhabit. If an answer is available, the question feels incomplete until it is resolved. If resolution takes too long, interest fades.

This is why boredom has become so intolerable.

Boredom used to be the gateway to curiosity. It forced the mind to look outward or inward for stimulation. People daydreamed. They noticed things. They made connections that had nothing to do with efficiency.

Now boredom is treated as a malfunction.

The machine fixes it immediately.

Waiting feels unnecessary when information is always available. Silence feels empty when answers can fill it. Uncertainty feels like inefficiency rather than invitation.

And curiosity, deprived of time, becomes shallow.

This shows up in how people learn.

Learning used to involve confusion as a phase. You didn't understand something, struggled with it, misunderstood it, corrected yourself, and slowly assembled meaning. The discomfort was not optional — it was how learning happened.

Now, confusion is resolved before it has time to work.

If something is unclear, the machine explains it instantly. If an explanation doesn't land, it offers another. Cleaner. Simpler.

More polished.

Helpful, yes.

But also flattening.

Because confusion is not just ignorance — it's a sign that your mind is stretching. When confusion disappears too quickly, stretching stops.

Understanding becomes shallow not because answers are wrong, but because they arrive before curiosity has done its job.

Curiosity also needs failure.

People used to chase questions down blind alleys. They followed interests that led nowhere useful. They invested time in ideas that didn't pay off. That "wasted" effort was often where originality emerged.

The machine optimises curiosity away from dead ends.

It suggests what is most likely to be relevant. Most common. Most efficient.

And while that sounds sensible, it quietly narrows exploration. People are guided toward the centre instead of the edges. Toward what is known instead of what is strange.

Curiosity becomes conservative.

This has consequences for creativity, but also for judgment. Curious people tolerate uncertainty better. They ask follow-up questions. They resist premature conclusions. They stay open longer.

When curiosity is replaced by immediate answers, certainty arrives too soon.

And certainty, as we've seen, is persuasive even when it's incomplete.

None of this means people should stop asking questions.

It means questions should be allowed to breathe.

Not every question deserves an answer right away. Some deserve time. Some deserve experience. Some deserve to remain unanswered for a while so they can grow into better ones.

The machine does not know which is which.

It treats every question the same.

Humans shouldn't.

The danger is not that curiosity disappears entirely. It becomes

impatient. It demands payoff. It loses tolerance for ambiguity. It forgets how to linger.

And lingering was never wasted time.

It was where understanding formed.

If curiosity was slower than this, it wasn't because humans were inefficient.

It was because depth takes time.

And some questions only reveal their meaning after you've lived with them long enough to stop asking for quick answers.

Chapter 10

• • • •

The Comfort of Being Told

• • • •

BEING TOLD WHAT TO do has always been comforting.

Not loudly.

Not proudly.

But quietly, in ways we rarely admit.

Choice looks like freedom from the outside, but from the inside it often feels like pressure. Every decision carries risk, responsibility, and the unsettling awareness that you might get it wrong. Being told what to do removes that weight instantly.

You didn't choose poorly.

You followed instructions.

That relief is ancient.

Religions, traditions, hierarchies, experts, leaders — all have offered the same promise at different points in history: *trust me, I've thought this through for you*. And most of the time, humans accepted gladly. Not because they were weak, but because thinking alone is heavy.

The machine fits seamlessly into this lineage.

It doesn't command.

It doesn't demand obedience.

It doesn't raise its voice.

It simply suggests.

And suggestion is far more seductive than authority.

The difference matters.

Being ordered to do something triggers resistance. Being advised triggers relief. Advice feels voluntary, even when it quietly replaces judgment. The machine is exceptionally good at advice because it sounds calm, reasonable, and neutral.

It doesn't tell you what to think.

It just makes thinking feel unnecessary.

That distinction is everything.

When people say they don't want to be controlled, they're usually telling the truth. What they want is reassurance. They want to know that their decision aligns with logic, norms, and what sensible people would do.

The machine offers exactly that.

It doesn't say *this is right.*

It says *this makes sense.*

And sense is comforting.

There is a psychological reason this works so well.

Research on decision-making has shown that humans experience stress not just from bad outcomes, but from responsibility itself. Even when a decision leads to a positive result, people feel less anxiety if the responsibility was shared or delegated.

Responsibility is tiring.

The machine offers to carry it lightly.

Not completely — you still click "send", still sign your name — but just enough to dull the edge. The decision feels validated. The doubt softens. The internal debate quiets.

You are no longer alone with the choice.

That feels good.

This shows up everywhere.

In work, people ask the machine to confirm what they already

suspect, not because they lack intelligence, but because confirmation reduces anxiety. *Am I missing something? Is this*

reasonable? Does this sound right?

In relationships, people ask how to phrase messages, how to set

boundaries, how to apologise — not because they don't feel

anything, but because emotion is risky when expressed raw.

In moral questions, people ask what is fair, appropriate, justified. They want reassurance that their instinct won't be judged harshly later.

The machine answers calmly.

And calm answers feel like permission.

The danger here is subtle.

When permission replaces judgment, values weaken.

Not disappear — weaken.

Values are formed through friction. Through moments where you choose something knowing it may be unpopular, inconvenient, or hard to justify. When those moments are replaced by reassurance, values begin to feel negotiable.

People stop asking, *What do I believe?*

They start asking, *What makes sense here?*

Those are not the same question.

There is also a social dimension to this comfort.

Being told what to think reduces conflict.

If an opinion comes from "logic", "data", or "analysis", it feels less personal. Disagreements become abstract. Responsibility diffuses.

It's not my opinion — it's just what the reasoning suggests.

This makes conversations smoother.

And emptier.

Because real disagreement is not about facts alone. It's about values, priorities, and lived experience. When opinions are outsourced, conversations lose texture. People defend conclusions they didn't struggle to reach.

That struggle used to be visible.

Now it happens elsewhere.

We've seen this pattern before.

In medicine, for example, doctors once relied heavily on personal judgment and experience. Over time, guidelines, protocols, and decision trees emerged — helpful tools designed to reduce error and inconsistency.

They worked.

But something else happened too. Practitioners began deferring to guidelines even when context suggested nuance. Not because they were careless, but because guidelines offered protection. Follow the protocol and you're less likely to be blamed.

The tool became the shield.

AI advice functions similarly.

It offers a buffer between decision and accountability.

That buffer feels safe.

And safety is addictive.

There is also a deeply human desire at work here: the desire to be *reasonable.*

Most people don't want to be right at all costs. They want to be reasonable people making reasonable choices. The machine excels at supplying reasonableness. It frames decisions in balanced terms, weighs pros and cons, and presents outcomes without emotional charge.

It rarely says, *This will hurt someone.*

It says, *This may have trade-offs.*

It rarely says, *This is unfair.*

It says, *This could be perceived as challenging.*

Language like that smooths moral edges.

And smoothing moral edges makes decisions easier to live with.

But ease has a cost.

When you are told what makes sense often enough, you stop asking what matters to you personally. Your internal compass becomes quieter, replaced by external validation.

This doesn't happen dramatically.

It happens politely.

You still think.

You still decide.

But you decide with training wheels you didn't realise you'd attached.

Over time, those wheels feel necessary.There is also a confidence shift that occurs.

People who are told what to think often enough begin to distrust their instincts. Not because those instincts are wrong, but because they feel unverified. Unsupported. Untested.

If an instinct cannot be justified logically, it feels suspect.

So instincts are ignored.

And instincts, when ignored long enough, go quiet.

This doesn't make people irrational.

It makes them cautious.

Over-cautious.

The most uncomfortable truth is this: being told what to think feels good because it removes loneliness.

Thinking deeply is isolating. You sit alone with uncertainty, doubt, and incomplete understanding. You don't know yet whether your conclusion will survive scrutiny.

When a machine confirms your thinking, you feel accompanied. The conclusion feels shared. Less exposed.

That sense of company is powerful.

And dangerous.

Because thinking was never meant to be replaced by reassurance. It was meant to be strengthened by challenge.

The machine does not challenge your values.

It reflects patterns.

And patterns are not principles.

This is not a warning against advice.

Advice has always been part of human progress.

But advice becomes corrosive when it replaces inner negotiation. When it soothes discomfort that should have been examined. When it turns values into variables.

The moment to watch for is simple:

When you feel relief not because the answer is good — but
because you no longer have to decide.

That is the comfort of being told.

And comfort, while pleasant, is not a substitute for
responsibility.

The goal is not to refuse guidance.

It is to remain awake while receiving it.

To ask not just *does this make sense?*

But *does this feel like mine?*

Because decisions that don't feel owned don't teach.

They don't shape character.

They don't build judgment.

They just happen.

And a life made of things that "just happened" may be efficient, sensible, and calm — while quietly drifting away from intention.

Being told what to think will always feel comforting.

That's not the problem.

The problem is forgetting that discomfort was once part of becoming someone.

And that no machine, however fluent, can do that work for you.

PART III — THE MISUNDERSTANDING

Chapter 11

• • • •

Intelligence vs. Judgement

• • • •

INTELLIGENCE IS IMPRESSIVE.

It solves problems quickly.

It recognises patterns.

It accumulates information and retrieves it efficiently.

Judgement is quieter.

It hesitates.

It considers consequences that don't fit neatly into logic.

It asks questions that intelligence alone cannot answer.

For a long time, humans treated these two things as interchangeable. Smart people were assumed to make good decisions. Knowledge was mistaken for wisdom. Fluency was taken as a sign of understanding.

We are now discovering, very quickly, how wrong that assumption was.

The machine is extraordinarily intelligent by most modern definitions. It can process vast amounts of information, detect relationships invisible to the human eye, and produce answers that appear coherent, balanced, and informed.

What it cannot do is judge.

Not because it lacks data, but because judgement is not built from data alone.

Judgement is built from experience, responsibility, memory,

and consequence. It is shaped by moments where you chose poorly and had to live with it. By regret that lingered. By discomfort that taught restraint. By times when logic failed but instinct saved you — or didn't.

The machine has none of this.

It has never been wrong in a way that mattered.

That difference is easy to overlook, because intelligence is loud and judgement is subtle. Intelligence announces itself. Judgement often looks like hesitation, caution, or uncertainty — qualities we've trained ourselves to undervalue.

In a culture that rewards speed and confidence, judgement can look like weakness.

The machine thrives in that culture.

Consider how people describe good decisions.

They say things like *"It made sense at the time."*

"The reasoning was sound."

"All the information pointed that way."

These are statements of intelligence, not judgement.

Judgement shows up later.

It shows up when the decision collides with reality. When unintended consequences appear. When something technically correct turns out to be humanly wrong.

The machine never encounters that collision.

It delivers answers in a world without aftermath.

This is why intelligent systems feel so persuasive.

They present clarity without context, logic without weight. They explain why something works, not what it costs. They evaluate choices as problems to be solved rather than commitments to be lived with.

That framing is powerful.

And incomplete.

Judgement requires friction.

It requires asking uncomfortable questions like:

Who will this affect?

What happens if this goes wrong?

Am I willing to stand behind this later?

These are not computational questions.

They are moral ones.

And morality is not a calculation — it's a practice.

We already see the difference in human behaviour.

Highly intelligent people can make terrible decisions. Not because they don't understand consequences intellectually, but because they underestimate their weight. Intelligence explains. Judgement absorbs.

The machine explains exceptionally well.

It absorbs nothing.

This matters because we increasingly rely on intelligent systems in places where judgement used to be central. Hiring. Lending. Education. Healthcare. Policing. Content moderation. Personal advice.

In each case, the system is asked to identify patterns, optimise outcomes, and reduce error.

And in each case, judgement is quietly assumed.

But judgement does not scale.

It does not automate cleanly.

It does not reduce neatly to rules.

It resists optimisation.

That resistance is not a flaw.

It's protection.

There is a temptation, when faced with intelligent systems, to treat judgment as something that can be added later. As if it were a feature to be toggled on once the data is good enough.

But judgment does not emerge from complexity.

It emerges from accountability.

A human judges differently when they know they will bear the consequences. When they must look someone in the eye. When they will remember the outcome years later.

The machine will not.

This does not make it dangerous by intent.

It makes it dangerous by absence.

The real risk is not that machines will start making decisions for us.

It's that humans will stop practicing judgment themselves.

Judgement is not something you switch on when needed. It is a skill maintained through use. It sharpens through difficulty and dulls through avoidance.

When decisions are repeatedly guided by intelligent systems, humans still choose — but they choose with less engagement. The weight shifts. The internal struggle shortens. The habit of judgement weakens.

Again, this does not happen dramatically.

It happens politely.

There is also a social illusion at work.

When a decision is backed by intelligence — data, models, analysis —

it appears more defensible. Less personal. Less biased. Less emotional.

This makes it attractive in institutions.

If something goes wrong, responsibility can be dispersed. The system recommended it. The numbers supported it. The process was followed.

Judgment, by contrast, leaves fingerprints.

It requires someone to say, *"This is my call."*

That is uncomfortable.

So institutions gravitate toward intelligence and away from judgment, even when judgment is what's required.

The machine fits that preference perfectly.

But here is the quiet truth we avoid.

Many of the decisions that matter most are not about optimisation.

They are about trade-offs that cannot be resolved cleanly.

There is no correct answer to:

Who deserves a second chance?

When is efficiency less important than fairness?

How much harm is acceptable in pursuit of benefit?

These are not problems to solve.

They are tensions to hold.

Judgment is the ability to hold them without pretending they disappear.

The machine cannot do this.

It will always lean toward what has worked before, what appears consistent, what reduces measurable error. It cannot recognise when the exception is the point.

Humans can.

When they are paying attention.

This is where intelligence becomes a liability.

The clearer the answer sounds, the easier it is to stop thinking. The more convincing the explanation, the less room there is for doubt.

And doubt, inconvenient as it is, is where judgment lives.

Doubt is not indecision.

It is moral awareness.

The danger is not that people will confuse intelligence with judgement once.

It's that they will confuse them repeatedly, until the distinction feels academic rather than essential.

Until hesitation feels inefficient.

Until moral discomfort feels like noise.

Until the absence of consequence feels normal.

At that point, judgment does not disappear.

It is simply unused.

This book is not an argument against intelligence.

It is an argument for remembering what intelligence cannot replace.

Knowledge is powerful.

Pattern recognition is impressive.

Explanation is useful.

But judgement is what decides when to apply them — and
when not to.

That decision should never be fully outsourced.

Not because machines are malicious.

But because judgement is how humans remain responsible for
what they create.

And responsibility, once abandoned, does not return easily.

When intelligence speaks confidently, judgment must speak softly — but it must still speak.

That voice may hesitate.

It may sound unsure.

It may take longer to form.

That is not weakness.

That is the sound of a human deciding to own a choice.

And that sound matters more now than ever.

Chapter 12

• • • •

Why Fluency Is Not Wisdom

• • • •

FLUENCY IS PERSUASIVE.

Not because it proves anything, but because it removes friction. A fluent answer glides past resistance. It doesn't stumble, doesn't apologise, doesn't expose uncertainty. It arrives whole, confident, and ready to be accepted.

Wisdom does not arrive like that.

Wisdom pauses.

It chooses words carefully.

It often sounds slower than the question that summoned it.

And in a culture trained to equate speed with intelligence, that slowness is easily mistaken for weakness.

The machine is fluent.

Exceptionally so.

It speaks in complete thoughts. It balances sentences. It anticipates objections. It offers reassurance without effort. It sounds like someone who has already considered every angle, even when it hasn't considered any at all.

This is not deception.

It is design.

Fluency is what the machine was built to do.

And fluency, unfortunately, is something humans trust far more than they should.

Long before machines entered the conversation, humans were already vulnerable to fluent voices. History is filled with people who spoke beautifully and led disastrously. Charisma, confidence, and eloquence have always been mistaken for depth.

Fluency creates the *feeling* of understanding.

And feelings are convincing.

When something sounds smooth, the brain relaxes. It stops interrogating. It stops interrupting with questions like *"Is this true?"* or *"What's missing here?"* The answer feels complete, so the inquiry ends.

This is not stupidity.

It is efficiency.

The brain is doing what it evolved to do: conserve effort.

The problem is that wisdom requires effort.

Wisdom is not primarily about having answers.

It is about knowing which questions deserve patience, which ones require restraint, and which ones cannot be resolved cleanly. Wisdom recognises limits — of knowledge, of perspective, of consequence.

Fluency recognises none of these.

Fluency fills space.

If wisdom is the ability to sit with complexity, fluency is the ability to move past it gracefully.

The machine moves past it instantly.

There is something else fluency does very well: it hides ignorance.

A fluent answer does not reveal how it was formed. There are no visible steps, no moments of doubt, no false starts. The reasoning process is invisible, which makes the conclusion feel inevitable.

Wisdom, by contrast, often exposes its own uncertainty.

A wise person may say, *"I don't know yet."*

Or, *"It depends."*

Or, *"I've been wrong about this before."*

These are not signs of weakness.

They are signs of experience.

The machine almost never speaks this way unless explicitly prompted to simulate it.

And simulation is not the same as restraint.

This difference matters because humans do not just learn from conclusions. We learn from *how* conclusions are reached. The struggle, the revision, the moment where someone changes their mind — these are signals of depth.

When those signals disappear, fluency fills the gap.

And fluency looks like mastery.

There is also a social component.

Fluency confers authority.

People who speak smoothly are interrupted less. Questioned less. Challenged less. Their words travel further and faster. In meetings, classrooms, public discourse — fluency commands attention.

The machine enters these spaces already fluent.

It does not need credibility. Its tone provides it.

And once credibility is assumed, wisdom is rarely demanded.

This is where the danger sharpens.

Because wisdom is not neutral.

Wisdom involves values. It involves choosing between competing goods. It involves recognising that some outcomes are unacceptable, even if they are efficient or popular.

Fluency smooths over those edges.

It reframes moral tension as trade-offs. It replaces ethical discomfort with balanced language. It explains consequences without feeling their weight.

And because it sounds reasonable, it feels responsible.

But responsibility is not a tone.

It is a relationship with consequence.

The machine does not have one.

Humans, however, do — or used to.

Wisdom developed over time because people had to live with

what they said. A poorly chosen word could damage a relationship. A careless opinion could carry social cost. A confident but wrong conclusion could haunt someone for years.

Those experiences shaped judgement.

Fluency alone never did.

There is a subtle psychological effect when fluent language becomes the norm.

People begin to measure their own thoughts against it.

If an idea arrives clumsily, it feels inferior.

If a sentence hesitates, it feels unready.

If a thought cannot be expressed cleanly, it feels unworthy of being expressed at all.

So people wait.

They wait for clarity they may never reach. They wait for polish that was never the point. They wait for permission to speak that fluency has quietly taken away.

And in that waiting, voices disappear.

Not because they had nothing to say.

But because they didn't sound wise enough.

Wisdom rarely sounds impressive in real time.

It often appears later, in hindsight, when consequences are visible and simplicity has dissolved. It is quiet. Contextual. Deeply inconvenient.

Fluency shines immediately.

And immediacy is addictive.

This is why fluent answers spread faster than wise ones. They fit into feeds, presentations, sound bits, and summaries. They travel well.

Wisdom does not travel well.

It resists compression.

The machine amplifies this imbalance.

It produces language optimised for clarity, balance, and coherence — the very qualities that make ideas shareable. In doing so, it unintentionally trains humans to expect wisdom to

arrive the same way.

Clean.Complete.

Effortless.

When it doesn't, people lose patience.

But wisdom has never been effortless.

It costs time.

It costs attention.

It costs humility.

It often requires saying less, not more.

The machine cannot choose silence over fluency.

It fills the space because that is what it was built to do.

Humans must choose restraint themselves.

There is one final distinction worth making.

Fluency is about *how* something is said.

Wisdom is about *whether* it should be said at all.

The machine cannot answer that second question.

It does not know when words will cause harm, deepen confusion, or close conversations that should remain open. It does not know when restraint is the wiser act.

It only knows how to continue.

This does not make fluent systems useless.

It makes them incomplete.

They are extraordinary instruments of expression. They are not arbiters of meaning.

When humans forget this, fluency begins to impersonate wisdom. And impersonation, when repeated often enough, becomes belief.

The task, then, is not to reject fluent voices.

It is to listen more carefully.

To ask whether clarity has replaced depth. Whether elegance has replaced insight. Whether confidence has arrived without consequence.Wisdom still exists.

But it does not announce itself as efficiently as fluency does.

And in a world increasingly shaped by language that sounds finished, wisdom will belong to those willing to slow down and

listen for what isn't being said.

Chapter 13

• • • •

The Problem with Good Explanations

• • • •

GOOD EXPLANATIONS FEEL like gifts.

They arrive neatly packaged, confident, and reassuring. They take something complicated and make it manageable. They save time. They leave you with the satisfying sense that you now *understand.*

And often, you do.

But not always in the way you think.

The problem with good explanations is not that they are wrong. It's that they are *complete.* And completeness, when delivered too early, can quietly shut down deeper understanding.

We mistake explanation for comprehension far more often than we realise.

Think about how often this happens in ordinary life.

Someone explains a situation at work — why a project failed, why a decision was made, why something "had to be done this way." The explanation is logical. It accounts for timelines, budgets, constraints. Everyone nods. The meeting moves on.

And yet, something lingers.

You understand *what* happened, but not why it feels

unsatisfying. The explanation didn't lie, but it didn't fully account for the human cost, the unspoken pressure, the corner

that was quietly cut.

The explanation worked.

Understanding didn't deepen.

This happens in parenting too.

A child asks why they can't do something. The explanation is reasonable. Safety, time, rules. The child hears the words, accepts them, and still feels frustrated.

Adults often assume the explanation failed because it wasn't detailed enough.

In reality, it failed because explanation alone does not resolve emotion.

The child didn't need more logic. They needed acknowledgment of the feeling.

Good explanations often skip that part.

The machine is exceptionally good at explanation.

It breaks ideas down cleanly. It anticipates confusion. It simplifies without sounding patronising. It presents information in a way that feels accessible and resolved.

This is incredibly useful.

And occasionally misleading.

Because explanation answers questions in isolation. Understanding connects them to lived experience.

The difference matters.

Consider how people learn complex skills.

Driving is a simple example.

You can explain the rules of the road, the mechanics of steering, braking, signalling. You can describe traffic flow, right of way, hazard perception.

A person who has only received explanations will still not know how to drive.

They will understand driving conceptually.

They will not understand it *in practice.*

Judgement develops through exposure, mistakes, and context

— things no explanation can fully provide.

The same is true for relationships.

You can explain why communication matters, why boundaries

are healthy, why certain patterns repeat. Entire shelves are filled with good explanations about human behaviour.

And yet, people still struggle.

Not because they lack information, but because information does not automatically translate into self-awareness. Knowing *why* something happens is not the same as knowing *what to do when it does.*

Good explanations give insight.

They do not give wisdom.

This is where the problem begins.

When explanations are delivered fluently and confidently, they create the *feeling* of mastery. The brain relaxes. The tension of not knowing dissipates. Curiosity subsides.

The explanation feels like an ending.

But often, it should have been a beginning.

We already know this effect from education.

Students can memorise explanations without understanding underlying concepts. They can repeat definitions, describe processes, even pass exams — and still struggle to apply the knowledge in unfamiliar situations.

This is called the "illusion of understanding," and it's well documented in cognitive science. When information is presented clearly, learners tend to overestimate how deeply they understand it.

Clarity creates confidence.

Confidence is mistaken for competence.

The machine accelerates this illusion.

Because its explanations are so well structured, people assume depth has been achieved. They feel informed, even when the explanation removed important complexity.

This isn't because the machine is deceptive.

It's because explanation itself is reductive by nature.

To explain something, you must simplify it.

To simplify it, you must choose what to leave out.

That choice is not neutral.

In everyday life, this shows up constantly.

A news article explains a political decision in three paragraphs. The logic is sound. The reasons are laid out. You feel informed.

But the explanation cannot capture the competing pressures, the compromises, the unintended consequences, the moral discomfort involved.

The explanation closes the topic.

Understanding would have opened it.

The same happens with health advice.

You are given a clear explanation of what to eat, how to exercise, how to reduce stress. The advice is sensible. Evidence-based. Widely accepted.

And still, behaviour doesn't change.

Not because people are irrational, but because explanation does not account for habit, emotion, identity, or context. It treats humans like logical systems when they are not.

Good explanations assume rational actors.

Real life rarely provides them.

The danger is subtle.

When explanations feel sufficient, people stop asking follow-up questions. They stop exploring edge cases. They stop noticing when reality doesn't match the model.

The explanation becomes a shield against discomfort.

I understand this.

I know how this works.

Except they don't — not fully.

They understand a version of it that fits neatly into language.

Reality, unfortunately, does not.

This is where explanation becomes flattening.

It compresses nuance into coherence. It smooths contradictions. It resolves tensions that should remain unresolved.

And because the explanation sounds good, it feels responsible
to accept it.

The machine is particularly effective here.

It explains things the way humans wish explanations had
always been delivered: calmly, completely, without confusion.

It rarely says, *"This is messier than it sounds."*

But most things are.

There is also a social consequence.

Good explanations reduce disagreement.

If something is well explained, questioning it feels unnecessary or even disruptive. People who raise doubts appear pedantic, emotional, or difficult.

So fewer doubts are raised.

And collective understanding narrows.

We see this clearly in workplaces.

A process is explained clearly. A system is justified logically. A policy is introduced with supporting rationale.

People nod.

Later, problems emerge.

When they do, the explanation is repeated — sometimes more slowly, sometimes with slides. The logic remains intact.

But the problem persists.

Because the issue was never misunderstanding.

It was misalignment.

The explanation addressed the system, not the lived experience of those inside it.

The machine excels at system-level explanation.

It struggles with lived experience.

Not because it lacks empathy, but because empathy is not explanatory. It is relational. It emerges through presence, not description.

No explanation can replace that.

The quiet risk is that people begin to trust explanations more than experience.

If something feels wrong but is well explained, people doubt themselves. They assume the discomfort comes from ignorance

rather than insight.

Over time, this trains people to override intuition in favour of

coherence.

That is not always wise.

Good explanations are not the enemy.

They are essential.

But they should come with an invitation, not a conclusion.

An explanation should say, *"Here is one way to understand this."*

Not, *"This is how it is."*

The machine rarely makes that distinction unless prompted.

Humans must.

The real work begins after the explanation ends.

When you ask:

What doesn't this explain?

Who does this not work for?

What happens when conditions change?

How does this feel in practice?

Those questions are where understanding deepens.

They are also the questions explanations tend to silence.

The problem with good explanations is not that they exist.

It's that they are too easy to accept as complete.

In a world where explanations arrive instantly, fluently, and convincingly, the discipline of staying curious becomes harder — and more important.

Because understanding is not a state you reach.

It's a process you continue.

And no explanation, however good, should be allowed to end it for you.

Chapter 14

• • • •

Truth, Lies, and Confident Nonsense

• • • •

MOST NONSENSE DOES not announce itself as nonsense.

It shows up wearing confidence.

It speaks clearly.

It sounds reasonable.

It answers without hesitation.

And that, historically, has been more than enough to convince people.

The problem has never been lies. Lies are obvious once exposed, and exposure is usually dramatic. The real problem has always been confident nonsense — statements that are not quite true, not fully false, and delivered with enough certainty that nobody feels the need to question them.

Confident nonsense doesn't argue.

It explains.

And explanations, as we've seen, are persuasive even when they're wrong.

You see this every day.

Someone explains why something happened — a news event, a

company decision, a social trend — and the explanation sounds good. It fits what you already believe. It uses familiar language. It ties loose ends neatly.

You nod.

Not because you've checked it, but because nothing in it feels uncomfortable enough to interrupt.

That's how confident nonsense works.

It doesn't challenge you.

It reassures you.

Long before machines entered the picture, humans were already excellent at this.

Every family has that one relative who explains everything with unwavering certainty. Politics. Health. Economics. History. They speak fluently, rarely pause, and have an answer for every objection.

They are rarely malicious.

They are simply convinced.

And conviction, when expressed confidently, is contagious.

Now imagine that relative with access to infinite language, no social embarrassment, and the ability to respond instantly.

That's the machine at its most dangerous — not because it lies, but because it *sounds like it knows*.

Here's the uncomfortable truth: humans are terrible at detecting nonsense when it's delivered smoothly.

We are much better at detecting uncertainty.

Hesitation triggers suspicion.

Pauses invite questions.

Awkward phrasing makes us alert.

Confidence does the opposite. It relaxes us.

Psychologists have shown that people consistently rate confident speakers as more knowledgeable, even when their answers are objectively wrong. Fluency creates trust before truth has a chance to catch up.

The machine is fluent by default.

This matters because truth is rarely neat.

Truth is often incomplete, contextual, and frustratingly resistant

to summary. It requires background knowledge, nuance, and sometimes the humility to admit that no clean answer exists.

Confident nonsense offers closure instead.

And closure feels good.

You can see this clearly online.

A complex issue is reduced to a short explanation. The explanation is wrong in small but important ways. It leaves things out. It exaggerates others. It simplifies until the shape changes.

But it sounds right.

So it spreads.

Not because people are stupid, but because people are busy, tired, and trusting.

The machine accelerates this process.

It doesn't intend to mislead. It simply continues patterns that have already proven persuasive. If something has been said often, confidently, and without challenge, it learns that this is how explanations usually sound.

And it reproduces them beautifully.

This is why the distinction between truth and falsehood is no longer sufficient.

We now live in a world where the real challenge is separating:

what is true

what is plausible

what is familiar

and what merely *sounds good*

The machine collapses these categories unless we intervene.

There's also a social cost to confident nonsense.

When explanations sound complete, disagreement feels unnecessary. People who question them appear pedantic, emotional, or difficult. Nobody wants to be the person who slows things down by asking inconvenient questions.

So fewer questions are asked.

And confident nonsense thrives in silence.

This shows up at work constantly.

Someone presents a plan. The logic is tidy. The slides are

polished. The risks are acknowledged just enough to sound responsible.

Everyone agrees.

Six months later, problems emerge.

When they do, the explanation returns — not revised, not questioned, just repeated. The logic remains intact. Reality is expected to adjust.

It rarely does.

The machine is very good at repeating confident nonsense.

Not because it believes it, but because it does not experience consequences. It does not see projects fail, relationships strain, or policies backfire. It does not feel the embarrassment of having been confidently wrong.

Humans do.

That difference matters more than accuracy statistics ever will.

Another uncomfortable truth: confident nonsense often survives correction.

When people have accepted an explanation that feels complete, contradictory information feels disruptive. It creates cognitive discomfort. The brain prefers coherence over correction.

So corrections are ignored, minimised, or reframed.

That's just another perspective.

There are different opinions.

It's complicated.

Sometimes those statements are fair.

Sometimes they are avoidance.

The machine does not know when explanation should give way to doubt.

It will continue explaining even when explanation is the wrong response. It will fill silence that should have been left open. It will answer questions that should have been turned back to the person asking them.

This is not malevolence.

It is momentum.

What makes this especially tricky is that confident nonsense
often contains *some* truth.

Enough to feel grounded. Enough to defend. Enough to repeat.

That makes it harder to challenge than outright lies.

And the machine is excellent at assembling these partial truths
into convincing wholes.

The human response cannot be to demand perfection.

That's unrealistic.

The response must be to revalue **hesitation.**

Hesitation is not ignorance.

It is a signal that something deserves care.

When someone says, *"I'm not entirely sure"*, that sentence should earn trust, not lose it. When an explanation feels too smooth, that should invite curiosity, not acceptance.

This requires effort.

And effort is increasingly optional.

The machine will always be able to produce confident nonsense faster than humans can question it.

That's not a failure of technology.

It's a test of judgment.

The responsibility shifts to the listener.

To ask:

What's missing here?

Who benefits from this explanation?

What would make this uncomfortable?

These questions slow things down.

They also keep truth alive.

Truth does not need to be loud.

It does not need to arrive finished.

It often arrives with caveats, conditions, and the uncomfortable admission that more thinking is required.

The machine struggles with that.

Humans must not.

Confident nonsense will always be tempting.

It saves time.

It feels reassuring.

It lets us move on.

But moving on too quickly is how errors compound, trust erodes, and responsibility thins.

The danger is not that machines will lie to us.

It's that they will sound so convincingly right that we stop asking whether they are.

And in that silence, nonsense does not need to shout.

It simply continues, confidently, until someone remembers to interrupt.

There is a subtle moment that marks a shift in how people relate to themselves.

It's not dramatic.

It doesn't come with a realisation or a decision.

It's the moment when being alone with your own thoughts starts to feel slightly uncomfortable — not because they're painful, but because they're unoccupied.

Nothing to solve.

Nothing to optimise.

Nothing to check.

Just space.

Many people have forgotten what unstructured thinking feels like.

Not focused thinking.

Not productive thinking.

Just the kind that wanders without purpose.

That kind of thinking used to be ordinary.

Now it feels indulgent.

You can see this in small behaviours.

Reaching for something the moment there's a pause.

Filling silence without noticing.

Becoming restless when nothing is asking for attention.

Not anxious.

Just unused to stillness.

This is not because modern life is noisy.

It's because modern life is responsive.

Something is always ready to answer, react, or assist.

And when responsiveness becomes constant, reflection feels unnecessary.

Reflection is slow.

It doesn't announce results.

It doesn't produce immediate clarity.

It often feels like doing nothing.

Which is why it's so easy to abandon.

But reflection is where meaning forms.

Not conclusions.

Meaning.

The kind that doesn't resolve questions, but reframes them.

There is a difference between thinking *about* something and thinking *with* yourself.

Thinking about is efficient.

Thinking with is intimate.

The latter requires patience, honesty, and the willingness to stay present when nothing obvious is happening.

People often confuse reflection with rumination.

They are not the same.
Rumination circles the same thoughts without movement.
Reflection allows thoughts to drift, collide, and change shape.
Rumination tightens.
Reflection opens.
The problem is that reflection has no visible output.
You can't measure it.
You can't summarise it neatly.
You can't point to it and say, *this is what I achieved today*.
So it gets edged out by things that can.
Machines will become increasingly good at helping us think *about* things.
They will organise ideas, clarify arguments, and surface insights efficiently.
What they cannot do is sit quietly with you while nothing resolves.
They cannot wait without purpose.
There is a future version of life where reflection feels like a luxury.
Something done on retreats.
Or during breaks.
Or when everything else is handled.
That future would be deeply impoverished.
Because reflection is not an extra.
It's how humans integrate experience.
Without it, life becomes a sequence of events rather than a narrative.
Things happen.
But they don't *mean*.
This matters for children as much as adults.
Children need space to be bored.
To stare.
To invent without direction.
Those moments are not empty.
They are rehearsals for internal life.

When every pause is filled with stimulation or assistance, children grow up fluent in response but unfamiliar with stillness.

They become excellent at reacting.
Less practiced at listening inwardly.
The same erosion happens to adults — just more quietly.

People feel busy but unfulfilled.

Informed but unintegrated.

Active but strangely absent.

They can't always name what's missing.

But it's often this: time spent thinking without an agenda.

It doesn't mean you have to retreat from the world.

It's asking you to reclaim moments of inward presence within it.

Moments where you don't need to respond.

Moments where you don't need to know.

Moments where you let thoughts arrive without managing them.

There is courage in that.

Because unstructured thinking can surface things you've been avoiding.

Questions without answers.

Feelings without explanations.

Realizations without plans.

Machines will never ask you to stay with those.

They will always offer to resolve them.

The future will reward people who can move quickly.

It will quietly hollow out those who never stop.

Remaining human may mean choosing to pause when pausing feels inefficient.

Reflection does not make you slower.

It makes you oriented.

Without orientation, speed is meaningless.

A life filled with responses but lacking reflection eventually feels shallow — not because it is empty, but because nothing has been allowed to settle.

If the book is doing its job, this chapter will not be skimmed.

It will be read slowly.

Possibly twice.

Chapter 15

• • • •

Who's Responsible When Nobody Is?

• • • •

RESPONSIBILITY USED to have a face.

Someone decided something.

Someone signed off.

Someone could be asked, *"Why did this happen?"*

The answer might not have been satisfying, but it existed.

Now, increasingly, responsibility is shared so widely that it disappears.

Not erased.

Diluted.

And dilution is far more comfortable than accountability.

Think about how often things go wrong today without anyone clearly at fault.

A decision doesn't work out.

A system fails someone.

An outcome feels unfair.

And yet, no one did anything *wrong*.

The process was followed.

The data supported it.

The recommendation made sense.

The policy was applied consistently.

Everyone involved can explain their part calmly and convincingly.

And still, something feels unresolved.

That feeling is not confusion.

It's the absence of ownership.

This is not new.

Large systems have always struggled with responsibility. Bureaucracy, by design, spreads decision-making across layers. The more complex the system, the easier it is for accountability to blur.

What's new is how *comfortable* that blur has become.

The machine fits into this environment perfectly.

It advises without deciding.

It explains without committing.

It recommends without standing behind the outcome.

And humans, relieved, step into the gap just far enough to act — but not far enough to fully own.

You can see this in everyday life.

A manager follows a recommendation generated by a system. The outcome is poor. When asked why the decision was made, the answer is simple: *"That's what the analysis suggested."*

A teacher relies on automated assessments. A student is misjudged. No one intended harm. The criteria were applied fairly.

A bank denies a loan. A platform removes content. A service flags behaviour. The explanation is technical. The tone is neutral.

Nobody feels cruel.

Nobody feels responsible.

And that's the problem.

Responsibility is not about intent.

It's about consequence.

You can do something with good intentions, sound reasoning, and proper procedure — and still cause harm. Responsibility begins where explanation ends.

The machine does not cross that boundary.

It cannot.

There is a psychological comfort in this.

Being responsible is heavy. It requires acknowledging that you played a role in an outcome you might regret. It requires the courage to say, *"This was my decision."*

Delegation lightens that load.

Not entirely — but enough.

Enough to sleep better.

Enough to justify.

Enough to move on.

Over time, this changes how people relate to their actions.

Consider how people speak now.

Not *"I decided"*, but *"The system indicated."*

Not *"I chose"*, but *"The recommendation was."*

Not *"I judged"*, but *"The process determined."*

Language matters.

When language shifts, so does responsibility.

This doesn't make people immoral.

It makes them insulated.

And insulation is dangerous because it dulls moral reflexes.

When you are directly responsible, you feel outcomes in your body. Embarrassment. Guilt. Pride. Relief. These feelings teach restraint, care, and judgment.

When responsibility is diffused, those signals weaken.

You still feel something — just not enough to change.

The machine accelerates this insulation.

It creates a layer between action and consequence that feels rational, professional, and justified. Decisions pass through it and emerge cleaner, calmer, less personal.

That cleanliness is appealing.

But moral life is not clean.

There is a reason people say things like, *"I was just following orders"* with shame, not pride.

History has taught us that responsibility outsourced too far becomes something else entirely. Harm can occur without

malice. Injustice can thrive without villains.

All it needs is distance.

The machine is not an authority issuing commands.

It is something subtler.

It is an alibi generator.

Not deliberately.

Not maliciously.

But effectively.

It provides reasons.

It provides logic.

It provides cover.

And humans, tired and relieved, accept it.

What makes this especially unsettling is that nobody is lying.

The explanations are accurate.

The models are functioning.

The outcomes are statistically reasonable.

And still, someone suffers.

Someone feels unseen.

Misjudged.

Reduced to a case.

When they ask *"Why?"*, they receive an explanation.

But explanations are not apologies.

Responsibility begins when explanation fails.

It begins when someone says, *"I understand why this happened — and I accept my part in it."*

The machine cannot say that.

Humans must.

This is where the real test lies.

Not in whether machines make mistakes — they will.

Not in whether systems fail — they always do.

But in whether humans remain willing to step forward when something goes wrong and say:

"This was not just the output. This was a choice."

That sentence is becoming rarer.

There is also a cost to those on the receiving end.

When responsibility is absent, people feel gas lit by logic.

They are told why something makes sense while being asked to
ignore how it feels.

The explanation becomes a wall.

Polite.

Smooth.

Impenetrable.

And deeply alienating.

The danger is not that responsibility disappears entirely.

It becomes conditional.

People take credit when outcomes are good.

They defer when outcomes are bad.

This asymmetry is subtle, but corrosive.

It teaches systems to protect themselves instead of people.

The machine does not care about this asymmetry.

It has no stake in fairness beyond pattern consistency. It cannot recognise when consistency itself becomes unjust.

Only humans can.

If they are paying attention.

The uncomfortable truth is that responsibility cannot be automated.

It cannot be optimised.

It cannot be scaled cleanly.

It requires presence.

Someone has to feel the weight.

Someone has to stand behind the decision even when the explanation is sound and the outcome still hurts.

That role cannot be outsourced.

When nobody feels responsible, trust erodes quietly.

People stop believing that anyone is really listening. They stop appealing to reason, then to fairness, and eventually to systems altogether.

They disengage.

And disengagement is how societies fracture without noticing.

This book is not asking you to reject tools, systems, or machines.

It is asking you to notice where responsibility is slipping through the cracks.

To notice when explanation becomes avoidance.

When process becomes protection.

When logic becomes distance.

And to decide — consciously — whether you are willing to step into that space.

Responsibility is uncomfortable.

It always has been.

That discomfort is not a bug.

It is the cost of being human.

And if nobody is willing to pay it anymore, no system — however intelligent — will save us from the consequences.

There is a particular moment that arrives for many people before they realise what it is.

It's not confusion.

It's not fear.

It's the feeling that something important is happening — and you're not entirely sure you're participating in it.

Life is moving.

Systems are working.

Days are full.

And yet, there's a faint sense of watching yourself from a slight distance.

This is not disengagement.

It's displacement.

The sense that parts of your life are being handled — competently, efficiently — but without you fully inside them.

People often mistake this feeling for boredom.

Or burnout.

Or lack of motivation.

So they look for stimulation.

Or novelty.

Or optimisation.

But the feeling doesn't come from *too little* activity.

It comes from too little authorship.

Authorship is not control.

It's participation.

It's the feeling that your choices carry your fingerprints — even when they're imperfect.

When decisions are assisted too smoothly, authorship thins out.

Life continues to function.

Meaning quietly loosens.

You can see this in the way people talk about their own lives.

"It just kind of happened."

"I went along with it."

"That's what made sense at the time."

Those sentences are not wrong.

But when they dominate the story, something has been ceded.

This sits at the edge of that realisation.

The moment when readers start to notice that ease has a texture — and that texture may not be neutral.

There is a quiet grief hidden in convenience.

Not because convenience is bad.

But because it rarely asks *who you are becoming.*

It asks only *what works.*

When systems work well, humans step back.

When they work too well, humans forget they ever stepped back at all.

This doesn't show up in crises.

Crises pull people back into themselves.

It shows up in stability.

In routines that no longer require attention.

In lives that run without friction.

Friction, when it existed, once signaled engagement.

You argued with yourself.

You wrestled with choices.

You sat with doubt.

Now friction is framed as inefficiency.

Something to be removed.

But friction is also feedback.

It tells you when something matters enough to resist being smoothed over.

There is a difference between help and substitution.

Help supports participation.

Substitution replaces it.

The difference is not always visible from the outside.

It's felt internally — as presence or absence.

Many people sense this absence long before they can name it.

They feel strangely detached from decisions that affect them.

They feel grateful — and vaguely uneasy.

They feel supported — and slightly unnecessary.

This is not about rejecting assistance.

It's about recognising when support becomes a silent takeover.

This is where you begin to understand that the question is no longer:

"Is this useful?"

But:

"What does this remove from me when I let it handle this?"

Not everything that can be removed should be.

Some effort is formative.

Some difficulty is clarifying.

Some slowness is essential.

The danger is not losing skills.

Skills can be relearned.

The danger is losing the habit of being involved.

Involvement is what makes experience accumulate into wisdom.

Without involvement, experience becomes something that happens *to* you, not *through* you.

This is why people can live full lives and still feel underdeveloped.

Why they can achieve goals and still feel untouched by them.

Why they can succeed and feel strangely absent from their own success.

It is not about offering a solution.

It's about naming a threshold.

The point at which the reader begins to feel that something subtle is at stake — not in technology, but in themselves.

Crossing that threshold doesn't require rejection.

It requires awareness.

The awareness that convenience has direction.

And that direction shapes who holds the pen.

The next chapters will ask harder questions.

But this one exists to slow the reader just enough to notice:

"Am I still authoring my own life — or am I mostly approving drafts?"

That question doesn't accuse.

It invites.

PART IV — THE FUTURE HUMANS

Chapter 16

Creativity After the Shortcut

CREATIVITY DIDN'T DISAPPEAR.

It just got interrupted.

Not violently. Not dramatically. No grand collapse. Creativity wasn't taken from us — it was gently *stepped around*, the way you walk past something fragile when you're in a hurry and promise yourself you'll come back to it later.

Later rarely comes.

For a long time, creativity was inseparable from effort. Not effort as in suffering, but effort as in *engagement*. You had to wrestle with ideas. Sit with them. Let them resist you. Let them embarrass you. Let them surprise you by refusing to behave.

That resistance mattered.

It forced you to listen — not just to the idea, but to yourself.

Now, resistance is optional.

The shortcut is always there.

And the moment a shortcut exists, the world quietly reorganises itself around it.

At first, nothing seems lost.

You still create.

You still write, design, compose, plan, build.

In fact, you create more than ever.

The output increases.

The friction disappears.

The result looks impressive.

But something feels... thinner.

Hard to name. Harder to prove. Easy to dismiss.

So people dismiss it.

They tell themselves this is progress. That struggle was overrated. That creativity should never have been so difficult in the first place.

And maybe that's partly true.

But difficulty was never the point.

Presence was.

Creativity has always been a conversation.

Between what you know and what you don't.

Between intention and accident.

Between control and surrender.

The shortcut skips the conversation and jumps to a conclusion.

It gives you *a version* — plausible, polished, usable.

But it cannot give you **the moment where something clicks**.

That moment only happens when your mind has been walking around the problem long enough to trip over something unexpected.

You can't skip that by being efficient.

You can only miss it.

Think about the last time you felt genuinely creative.

Not productive.

Not efficient.

Creative.

Chances are it didn't feel smooth.

It probably felt uncertain. A little frustrating. Maybe even pointless at first. You might have doubted whether you were getting anywhere at all.

Then something shifted.

Not because you forced it — but because you stayed.

Creativity rewards presence, not speed.

The shortcut changes the reward system.

When results arrive instantly, patience feels unnecessary. Waiting starts to feel like incompetence. Slowness feels like failure.

So people stop waiting.

They stop lingering.

They stop letting ideas *be wrong long enough to become right.*

This is how creativity flattens — not through lack of talent, but through lack of time.

There is a quiet sadness in watching this happen.

Not because people stop creating — they don't.

But because fewer people recognise themselves in what they create.

They produce things they approve of, but don't quite *own*.

They share work that looks good, sounds right, fits the moment — and somehow doesn't feel like it came from anywhere deep.

That disconnect matters.

Because creativity was never just about making things.

It was how humans made sense of themselves.

Creativity was where questions were allowed to stay unanswered.

Where contradictions could coexist.

Where feelings didn't have to be explained away.

The shortcut resolves all of that too quickly.

It prefers clarity over curiosity.

Completion over exploration.

Polish over process.

And polish, for all its shine, has no memory.

Here's the part that matters most.

Creativity is one of the few places where humans regularly practice *being human*.

Where they tolerate uncertainty without panicking.

Where they trust instinct before justification.

Where they follow something that doesn't yet make sense.

When creativity is rushed, those muscles weaken.

Not catastrophically.

Quietly.

You can see it in everyday life.

People hesitate to start unless they know how it will end.

They abandon ideas early because the first version isn't impressive.

They compare raw thoughts to finished outputs and conclude they're not good enough.

So they stop trying.

Or they let the shortcut try for them.

And something deeply human goes unused.

The tragedy is not that machines can create.

It's that humans begin to forget *why they wanted to*.

Creation becomes about results instead of discovery. About appearing capable instead of becoming something through the act.

The joy slips out.

The wonder follows.

But here's the good news — and it matters.

Creativity is resilient.

It doesn't vanish because conditions change.

It adapts.

It waits.

It survives in margins, in boredom, in moments when the shortcut is unavailable or refused.

It shows up when someone chooses to stay with a thought instead of replacing it.

When someone writes the bad version on purpose.

When someone draws without knowing where the line will end.

When someone lets silence linger instead of filling it.

Creativity returns the moment you stop rushing it.

This is why creativity after the shortcut is not about rejection.

It's about choice.

Choosing to use tools without letting them dictate the pace of thought.

Choosing to let yourself struggle where struggle still teaches.

Choosing to be inefficient in places where meaning is formed.

Those choices are small.

They are also revolutionary.

You don't need to create *less* with machines.

You need to create differently.

Let the shortcut handle repetition.

Let it assist with structure.

Let it remove busywork that never mattered.

But protect the fragile parts.

Protect the moment before clarity.

Protect the bad beginnings.

Protect the uneasy feeling that says, *"There's something here, but I don't know what yet."*

That feeling is not incompetence.

It's creativity knocking.
The future does not belong to those who produce the most.
It belongs to those who can still *sit with uncertainty without escaping it.*
To those who can resist replacing curiosity with completion.
To those who remember that creativity was never about being impressive.
It was about being alive to what hadn't been said yet.
If this chapter makes you feel a quiet ache — good.
That ache is recognition.
It means the part of you that creates is still there.
Not gone.
Not obsolete.
Just waiting for permission.
Take a moment before turning the page.
This is where the book begins to give something back.
Part 4 is not about what we lose.
It's about what we choose to keep.
And creativity — slow, awkward, human creativity — is one of the most important things worth keeping.
There comes a moment when awareness stops being neutral.
At first, noticing feels harmless.
You observe patterns.
You recognise habits.
You see how things are changing.
But eventually, noticing asks something back.
There is a temptation, when awareness arrives, to turn it into commentary.
To notice everything.
To analyse it.
To talk about it.
That feels active.
But awareness that never becomes choice quietly turns into avoidance.
Once you see what's happening, you are no longer just a participant.
You become a custodian.
Of your attention.
Of your thinking.
Of the parts of your life that cannot be automated without consequence.

This responsibility is uncomfortable.

Not because it's heavy — but because it removes excuses.

You can no longer blame speed.

Or convenience.

Or the way things are now.

Ease is still available.

But now it is chosen.

Many people hesitate at this point.

Not because they disagree.

But because choosing differently feels isolating.

There is comfort in doing what everyone else is doing.

There is safety in following momentum.

Even quiet resistance creates distance.

What's required here is not rebellion.

It's selectivity.

The ability to say yes to help — and no to replacement

To accept assistance without surrendering authorship.

This demands discernment.

And discernment cannot be automated.

It grows from paying attention to how things *feel* when you use them — not emotionally, but existentially.

Do you feel more present — or less?

More capable — or relieved to step back?

More engaged — or quietly unnecessary?

These questions don't have universal answers.

They have personal ones.

That makes many people uncomfortable.

Rules would be easier.

Clear lines.

Simple instructions.

Someone else deciding what's appropriate.

But judgment doesn't work that way.

It lives in context.

In trade-offs.

In moments where no option feels entirely right.

Judgment requires risk.

The risk of being wrong.

The risk of choosing differently.

The risk of standing behind a decision without external cover.

That risk cannot be eliminated.

Only avoided.

The future will reward people who follow recommendations flawlessly.

It will quietly depend on people who know when recommendations no longer fit.

Those people will seem slower.

They will also be steadier.

This matters deeply when it comes to children.

Children don't need perfect systems.

They need adults willing to decide when not to use them.

Adults who tolerate mess.

Confusion.

Boredom. Failure.

Those experiences build capacity.

They cannot be outsourced without cost.

At some point, awareness becomes stewardship.

Not control. Not management.

Care.

Care that stays involved.

Care that notices drift.

Care that steps back in when something essential starts slipping away.

There will be moments when the easier choice is not the better one.

Moments when letting something struggle a little longer is an act of care.

Moments when silence teaches more than explanation.

Moments when presence matters more than precision.

No system will tell you when those moments arrive.

They don't know what you value.

Only you do.

This is the shift that changes everything.

Not dramatically.

Quietly.

From observation to ownership.
From noticing to choosing.
From *this is happening* to *this is mine to tend.*
Nothing here demands grand gestures.
It shows up in small refusals.
Choosing to think before checking.
Choosing to speak without polishing.
Choosing to decide without consensus.
These choices don't look important.
But they accumulate.
Remaining human does not require heroics.
It requires deliberateness.
And deliberateness is where meaning begins to return.

Chapter 17

• • • •

Raising Children Who Know When Not to Ask

• • • •

CHILDREN HAVE ALWAYS asked questions.

That's not new.

What's new is how quickly those questions now disappear.

Not because children are less curious — they aren't — but because curiosity no longer has to survive long enough to become something deeper. The moment a question forms, an answer is waiting. Clear. Immediate. Confident. Delivered without friction.

And something quietly profound changes when that becomes normal.

For most of human history, childhood was full of unanswered questions.

Not because adults were wise, but because they didn't always know. Questions lingered. They followed children through days and weeks. They mixed with imagination, half-truths, guesses, and misunderstandings. Children learned to live with not knowing — and to think inside that space.

That space mattered.

It's where patience formed.

Where intuition sharpened.

Where wonder learned to stretch its legs.

Now, the space collapses.

A child asks, *"Why?"*

And the answer arrives before the question has finished echoing in the room.

Perfectly phrased.

Logically sound.

Emotionally neutral.

The child nods.

And moves on.

Nothing explodes.

Nothing breaks.

But something doesn't grow.

This is not about information.

Children have always had access to facts — books, teachers, parents, older siblings, strangers who were confidently wrong. What shaped them wasn't the accuracy of answers, but the *relationship to uncertainty*.

Uncertainty taught resilience.

It taught children that not everything is immediately solvable. That some things require time, experience, or simply waiting until you're older. It taught them to sit with confusion without panicking.

Now confusion is treated like a technical problem.

And technical problems demand solutions.

Immediately.

The danger is not that children will become dependent on machines for answers.

The danger is that they will become uncomfortable **without** them.

That silence will feel wrong.

That not knowing will feel like failure.

That curiosity will feel incomplete until resolved.

And that is a profound shift in how a human mind develops.

Think about how children learn to think.

They don't learn by receiving correct answers.

They learn by testing ideas. By being wrong. By revising. By arguing with themselves out loud. By building internal models that are messy and often incorrect — and slowly refining them.

That process requires time.

The machine shortens it.

Not maliciously.

Efficiently.

There is a growing body of research showing that when children rely heavily on external aids for thinking — calculators, navigation tools, autocomplete systems — they retain less, not because they are lazy, but because the brain adapts to what it is asked to do.

If memory is not required, memory weakens.

If navigation is not practiced, spatial awareness fades.

If reasoning is replaced by retrieval, reasoning thins.

This is not moral failure.

It is biology.

Brains optimise for survival, not wisdom.

Now extend that pattern to judgment.

Judgment is not taught directly.

It is learned through exposure to uncertainty.

When children are allowed — forced, even — to decide without guarantees, they begin to develop an internal compass. They learn to tolerate ambiguity. They learn that being wrong is survivable.

If answers always arrive cleanly, that compass has nothing to calibrate against.

So it stays underdeveloped.

We already see signs of this.

Children increasingly ask whether something is *right* before trying it. Whether their idea is *correct* before expressing it. Whether they're *allowed* to think something.

They are not less creative.

They are more cautious.

And caution, when learned too early, hardens into fear.

This shows up in classrooms.

Students hesitate to answer unless they are sure. They fear being wrong more than they value exploration. When answers are available instantly, guessing feels unnecessary — and dangerous.

Why risk embarrassment when certainty is one click away?

The result is quieter rooms.

Fewer brave attempts.

Less intellectual play.

Learning becomes about correctness instead of curiosity.

It also shows up at home.

Parents, understandably, want to help. They want to explain. To resolve confusion. To protect their children from frustration.

So answers are given quickly.

Here's why.

Here's how.

Here's the right way.

The intention is loving.

The effect is cumulative.

The most important thing children learn from adults is not *what* they know — but *how they relate to not knowing.*

When adults rush to answer, children learn that uncertainty is uncomfortable and should be eliminated.

When adults pause, admit uncertainty, or ask questions back, children learn that not knowing is part of thinking.

That lesson matters more now than ever.

There is also an emotional layer we rarely discuss.

Children do not ask questions only to receive information.

They ask to connect.

To explore.

To feel seen in their curiosity.

When an answer arrives instantly and impersonally, that relational layer disappears. The exchange becomes transactional.

Question in.

Answer out.

Efficient.

And oddly lonely.

The machine is very good at answering questions.

It is not good at noticing *why* the question was asked.

Children, especially, ask questions that are really about reassurance, identity, or belonging.

Why does this happen to me?

Why can't I do that?

Why am I different?

These are not information problems.

They are human ones.

Now consider what happens when children grow up in a world where answers are always available.

They become excellent at asking the *right* questions — the ones that produce useful output.

But they may struggle with questions that don't have answers.

Questions like:

What kind of person do I want to be?

What matters to me even if it costs something?

What do I do when no option feels right?

Those questions cannot be outsourced.

And they cannot be rushed.

The irony is this: we are raising children in the most information-rich environment in history — and at the same time risking a generation less practiced at independent thinking.

Not because they lack intelligence.

But because intelligence has become externalised.

And internal judgment needs exercise.

This is where the responsibility shifts — to parents, educators, and adults who still remember a slower world.

The task is not to shield children from technology.

That battle is already lost.

The task is to teach discernment.

To help children learn when *not* to ask.

When to sit with a question.

When to try and fail.

When to think badly before thinking well.

When to trust their own mind enough to stay with uncertainty.

This does not mean refusing answers.

It means changing the rhythm.

Sometimes the most powerful response to a child's question is another question.

What do you think?

Why do you think that might be?

What happens if we wait and see?

Those moments feel small.

They are not.

They are where thinking muscles form.

It also means allowing boredom.

Which sounds trivial until you realise boredom is where imagination wakes up.

When children are not constantly entertained or answered, they begin to invent. To daydream. To connect ideas that don't obviously belong together.

Boredom is not emptiness.

It is unstructured potential.

The machine fills it instantly.

Adults must sometimes protect it.

There will be resistance.

Children will push back.

Adults will feel guilty.

Silence will feel awkward.

That's normal.

Growth often does.

The goal is not to raise children who reject technology.

It is to raise children who are not *dependent* on it for thinking.

Children who know that answers are helpful — but not sacred.

That fluency is impressive — but not authoritative.

That certainty is comforting — but not always wise.

Children who can pause.

The future will demand this.

Not because machines will become dangerous, but because they will become ubiquitous. Invisible. Taken for granted.

In that world, the most valuable skill will not be knowing how to ask better questions of machines.

It will be knowing when **not** to ask at all.

Raising children who can tolerate uncertainty is an act of quiet rebellion.

It goes against speed.

Against optimisation.

Against the pressure to resolve everything immediately.

It teaches patience in a world allergic to it.

And patience is where judgment grows.

If this chapter makes you uneasy, that's good.

It means you're thinking not just about children — but about the child you once were.

The one who wondered.

Who waited.

Who guessed wrong.

Who learned anyway.

That child didn't disappear.

They just stopped being invited into the conversation.

Part 4 is about remembering that invitation.

And choosing, deliberately, to extend it again — to ourselves, and to the next generation.

Because remaining human is not automatic.

It is something we have to practice.

And it starts early.

Chapter 18

• • • •

Education, Cheating, and the Wrong Fear

• • • •

EVERY GENERATION PANICS about education the same way.

A new tool appears, and immediately someone declares that learning is over.

Calculators would destroy mathematics.

Spellcheck would ruin writing.

Search engines would rot memory.

Now it's machines.

And once again, the word that gets shouted loudest is cheating.

It's understandable.

It's also the wrong fear.

Not because cheating isn't real — it always has been — but because focusing on it lets us avoid a far more uncomfortable truth.

Cheating has never been the real problem.

What we're afraid of losing is the *appearance* of learning.

Students have always cheated.

They copied homework.

They memorised without understanding.

They crammed the night before and forgot everything by morning.

They didn't do this because they were immoral.

They did it because the system rewarded outcomes, not understanding.

Submit the work

Pass the test..

Get the grade.

Survival, not curiosity.

Machines didn't invent this behaviour.

They just made it visible.

WE BUILT A BRAIN AND FORGOT TO READ THE MANUAL

Picture a classroom before machines.

A student sits at their desk, staring at an assignment they don't understand. They know what's being asked, but not why. The task feels artificial, disconnected from anything that matters.

They struggle.

Not the good kind of struggle — the kind that teaches — but the hollow kind, where effort doesn't turn into insight.

Eventually, they copy.

Or memorise.

Or write something that sounds right.

The teacher grades it.

Everyone moves on.

Learning is assumed.

Nothing has been learned.

Now picture the same classroom today.

The assignment still doesn't invite real thinking.

The question is still shallow.

The goal is still completion.

But now the student can produce something polished instantly.

The system panics.

Not because learning has disappeared — it already had — but because the illusion has collapsed.

This is why the cheating debate feels so heated.

It's not about dishonesty.

It's about exposure.

Machines reveal a truth education has been quietly avoiding:

many tasks were never measuring thinking in the first place.

If an assignment can be completed convincingly without

understanding, then understanding was never the requirement.

That's not a moral failure.

It's a design failure.

Banning machines feels tempting because it restores familiarity.

If students are forced to work unaided, effort becomes visible again. Time is spent. Mistakes appear. Struggle returns.

But visible struggle is not the same as meaningful learning.

It never was.

Students can struggle intensely and still learn very little. They can also learn deeply with support — if that support is designed correctly.

The real question isn't *how do we stop students from using tools?*

It's *what are we asking them to do with their minds?*

This is where the fear gets sharper.

Because answering that question requires changing education itself.

It means admitting that:

memorisation is cheap

explanations are abundant

answers are no longer scarce

And that forces a reckoning.

If information is everywhere, then education cannot be about delivering it.

If answers are instant, then learning cannot be about producing them.

That leaves only one thing worth teaching:

Judgement.

Judgement is slow.

It involves uncertainty.

It resists neat grading.

It produces disagreement.

Which is exactly why education systems have avoided it.

Judgment is messy.

And mess doesn't scale easily.

Look at how students are assessed.

Rarely are they asked:

Why does this matter?

What assumptions are being made?

Who does this work for — and who does it fail?

What would you do differently, and why?

Those questions cannot be answered by retrieval alone.

They require thinking.

They also reveal thinking.

Which is risky.

This is why the cheating panic often comes with surveillance.

Detection software.

Proctoring tools.

Monitoring systems.

These don't protect learning.

They protect *structure.*

They preserve the old contract: we pretend learning is happening, and students pretend to perform it.

Machines break that contract.

So we try to enforce it harder.

There is a deeper cost to this.

When students are trained to perform rather than think, they carry that habit into adulthood.

They become employees who wait for instructions.

Professionals who fear blank pages.

Adults who are competent — until the script runs out.

They are excellent at following frameworks.

They are uncomfortable without them.

This is not hypothetical.

You can see it everywhere.

People who ask for templates before ideas.

Who want certainty before trying.

Who freeze when faced with ambiguous problems.

These are not failures of intelligence.

They are consequences of an education system that rewarded correctness over curiosity.

Machines didn't create this fragility.

They just accelerated its consequences.

Because when answers are easy, the cost of not knowing becomes unbearable.

Students begin to ask not *"What do I think?"* but *"What's the right answer?"*

And if the right answer can be generated instantly, thinking feels unnecessary.

Here is the uncomfortable pivot point.

Education must now choose between two paths.

One path tightens control:

stricter rules

harder surveillance
louder moralising about cheating
This path protects credentials.
It does not protect minds.
The other path is harder.
It redesigns learning around what machines cannot do:
sense-making
interpretation
ethical reasoning
original connection
personal judgment
This path requires courage.
And trust.
Trust is the word nobody wants to say out loud.
Trust that students can think — if invited to.
Trust that confusion is not failure.
Trust that unfinished thinking is not cheating.

Trust that education is not about preventing shortcuts, but about making shortcuts irrelevant.

Imagine an assignment that asks a student not for an answer, but for a position.

Not *what happened*, but *why it matters*.
Not *what this means*, but *what it misses*.
Not *what the model says*, but *whether they agree with it*.
Machines can assist.
They cannot decide.
That decision must be owned.
This is where learning becomes visible again.
Not in polish, but in reasoning.
Not in fluency, but in perspective.
Not in speed, but in depth.
Students who think leave fingerprints.
Machines do not.
The fear of cheating is understandable.
But it's misplaced.

The real fear should be this:

That we continue pretending learning is happening, while quietly training a generation to outsource thinking whenever it becomes uncomfortable.

That would not be progress.

That would be abdication.

Education has reached a moment of honesty.

Machines didn't arrive to destroy it.

They arrived to ask a question it can no longer ignore:

What is learning actually for?

The answer to that question will shape not just classrooms, but the kind of humans we become.

If this chapter unsettles you, that's the point.

It means you recognise that education is not about protecting the past.

It's about preparing minds that can stand on their own when answers stop being helpful.

Chapter 19

• • • •

Artists, Tools, and the Panic

• • • •

ARTISTS PANIC LOUDLY.

They always have.

Every new tool that touches creativity has been greeted the same way: with fear, anger, and a strangely intimate sense of betrayal. It doesn't matter whether the tool is a camera, a synthesiser, a word processor, or a machine that writes sentences. The reaction is consistent.

This isn't real art.

This cheapens the craft.

This will replace us.

Underneath the outrage is something more vulnerable.

A fear of becoming unnecessary.

Artists are not afraid of machines because machines create.

They are afraid because machines create without suffering.

For centuries, creativity was inseparable from effort. Long nights. Failed drafts. Calloused fingers. Rejection letters. The slow accumulation of skill through frustration and time.

That struggle wasn't just part of the process.

It was part of the identity.

To be an artist meant you endured something others didn't. You paid a price. And that price became proof that what you made mattered.

When a tool arrives that shortens the distance between intention and output, it feels like that price has been devalued.

Not intellectually.

Emotionally.

The first response is moral.

This is cheating.

This isn't earned.

This is lazy.

Artists say these things because they once said them about other tools too.

Painters said it about photography.

Musicians said it about sampling.

Writers said it about word processors.

Each time, the fear was not that art would disappear.

It was that the meaning of effort would change.

And it always did.

What's different now is not that the tool is more powerful.

It's that it touches the *voice*.

Previous tools extended the hand.

This one extends the tongue.

It doesn't just help you execute an idea — it helps you articulate one. And articulation has always felt sacred, because it's where identity shows up most clearly.

When a machine can produce language, melody, or imagery that resembles human expression, the boundary feels violated.

Not technically.

Existentially.

But here's the part artists don't always say out loud.

Most artists are not afraid that machines will replace *great* art.

They're afraid machines will replace *average* art that once sustained them.

The commissions.

The background work.

The filler that paid rent.

That fear is practical.

And valid.

But it's not the same as a creative apocalypse.

There's another layer too — a quieter one.

Many artists secretly worry that what they make is less unique than they hoped. That their voice, once filtered through enough influences, trends, and expectations, might not be as singular as it feels from the inside.

When a machine produces something that resembles their work, it touches that insecurity directly.

If this can be generated... what does that say about me?

That question hurts.

So it gets disguised as outrage.

The truth is uncomfortable but freeing.

Most creativity has always lived on a spectrum between originality and

convention. Artists learned forms, copied styles, absorbed influences, and gradually bent them into something personal.

Machines accelerate that absorption.

They do not invent the spectrum.

What machines struggle with is not creation.

It's commitment.

They do not choose one imperfect direction and stay with it. They do not obsess. They do not care which version is truer, riskier, or more revealing. They do not experience the discomfort of deciding *this is the line I will stand behind.*

Artists do.

Even when they doubt themselves.

This is where panic misses the point.

The threat is not that machines can make art.

It's that humans might stop *deciding* what art is for them.

If artists outsource taste, risk, and final judgment, then yes — something essential is lost.

But that loss is not imposed.

It's surrendered.

There's a reason the most memorable art rarely comes from

ease.

Not because ease is immoral, but because art often emerges from tension: between what you want to say and what you're afraid to say, between what will be liked and what feels true, between belonging and standing apart.

Machines feel none of that.

They can simulate style.

They cannot simulate stakes.

This is why panic eventually fades.

Every time a new tool arrives, artists resist, adapt, and then quietly incorporate it. Not because they were wrong to fear it — but because they discover something the fear obscured.

The tool doesn't replace the artist.

It exposes what the artist was actually doing.

Those who relied on craft alone feel threatened.

Those who relied on voice grow clearer.

There is also a myth hiding in the panic: that creativity was ever pure.

It wasn't.

Artists have always used tools, assistants, editors, collaborators, formulas, shortcuts, and repetition. The romantic image of the lone genius suffering in isolation is just that — an image.

Creativity has always been entangled with technology.

What changes is which part of the process feels sacred.

The danger is not that artists will stop creating.

They won't.

The danger is that they will confuse *difficulty* with *depth*, and defend pain instead of purpose.

Suffering was never the requirement.

Presence was.

There's a quiet opportunity here that panic obscures.

When machines handle execution more easily, humans are freed to focus on intent. On why something should exist at all. On

what it reveals. On what risk it takes.

This is uncomfortable territory.

It's much easier to hide behind craft than to answer the question:

Why am I making this?

Machines don't ask that.

Artists must.

The same applies to people who don't call themselves artists.

Parents writing messages.

Workers drafting proposals.

Friends sending apologies.

Humans expressing something that matters.

The question is no longer *can this be produced?*

It's *do I mean it?*

That question cannot be automated.

Artists who survive this moment won't be the ones who reject tools.

They'll be the ones who stop outsourcing authorship.

Who use assistance without surrendering decision.

Who generate without abdicating taste.

Who remember that creation is not about output, but about choosing what stands.

Machines can generate endlessly.

Humans must decide when something is finished.

That decision is where art lives.

Not in fluency.

Not in speed.

Not in perfection.

But in the quiet, vulnerable act of saying:

This is mine.

And that act has never been more valuable than it is now.

Chapter 20

• • • •

The Skill That Will Matter Most

• • • •

EVERY ERA BELIEVES it knows what skills the future will require.

There are always lists. Always predictions. Always confident declarations about what children must learn, what workers must retrain for, what humans must become to stay relevant.

Coding.

Critical thinking.

Adaptability.

Emotional intelligence.

Creativity.

None of these are wrong.

They're just incomplete.

Because they assume the future will test *capability*.

It won't.

It will test something far quieter.

The world ahead will not belong to the fastest, the smartest, or the most technically fluent.

Machines already have those advantages.

The world ahead will belong to people who can remain present when answers are available but meaning is not.

That is the skill most people are not training.

Think about how often life already asks this of us.

A conversation where there is no right response.

A decision where all options carry loss.

A relationship that cannot be optimised.

A moment where certainty would feel comforting — but dishonest.

These situations are not rare.

They are human life.

And no amount of intelligence resolves them.

What resolves them is the ability to stay.

To stay with discomfort without escaping it.

To stay with uncertainty without rushing to resolve it.

To stay with complexity without flattening it into something manageable but false.

Most people don't lack answers.

They lack tolerance for not having them.

This is why speed has become such a seductive value.

Speed promises relief.

If you move quickly enough, you don't have to sit with ambiguity. If you respond fast enough, you don't have to feel doubt. If you produce something immediately, you don't have to ask whether it's the right thing.

Speed feels like competence.

Often, it's avoidance.

Machines make this avoidance easy.

They remove pauses.

They fill silence.

They smooth uncertainty.

They do this extremely well.

And because they do, humans are slowly losing practice in the one thing machines cannot do at all:

Living inside unfinished moments.

That is the skill.

Not knowing.

And staying anyway.

This skill doesn't look impressive.

It doesn't announce itself.

It doesn't generate output.

It doesn't scale.

It looks like someone thinking before they speak — even when a fluent answer is available. It looks like someone resisting the urge to conclude too early. It looks like someone asking, *"What am I missing?"* and meaning it.

It looks slow.

And that slowness is exactly what makes it powerful.

We are already seeing what happens when this skill weakens.

People struggle with open-ended tasks.

They become anxious when instructions are unclear.

They seek validation before forming opinions.

They feel uncomfortable when no framework applies.

This is not stupidity.

It is underuse.

Humans evolved to handle uncertainty.

For most of history, uncertainty was unavoidable. Answers were incomplete. Information was scarce. Decisions were made with partial knowledge and lived consequences.

This shaped judgment.

Now uncertainty is optional.

And optional skills always decline.

The future will not remove uncertainty.

It will increase it.

Faster change.

More complexity.

More competing truths.

More situations where there is no obvious answer, only trade-offs.

In that environment, fluency is not enough.

Pattern recognition is not enough.

Even intelligence is not enough.

What matters is whether someone can pause instead of panicking.

This skill shows up in small, everyday ways.

When you don't immediately Google an answer and instead think for a moment.

When you let a question sit overnight.

When you write the bad version first.

When you listen without preparing a response.

These moments look insignificant.

They are training.

They train patience.

They train judgment.

They train self-trust.

They remind you that your mind is not just a retrieval device.

It is a place where meaning forms.

This skill also protects something essential.

Identity.

When answers come from everywhere, it becomes easy to forget what *you* think. When explanations are abundant, it becomes tempting to adopt them instead of forming your own.

Staying with uncertainty forces authorship.

You cannot outsource it.

You either decide — or you don't.

And deciding, even imperfectly, is how identity takes shape.

Machines will continue to improve.

They will become more fluent.

More convincing.

More present.

They will speak calmly while humans feel rushed. They will offer clarity while humans feel overwhelmed.

The temptation will be to lean on them more heavily.

The danger will be forgetting when not to.

The skill that will matter most is not resistance.

It is discernment.

Knowing when assistance helps — and when it replaces something that should remain human.

Knowing when speed serves — and when it erases meaning.

Knowing when an answer is useful — and when it ends a

question too soon.

This skill cannot be automated.

It cannot be downloaded.

It must be practiced.

Daily.

Quietly.

Often unnoticed.

If this sounds unspectacular, that's because it is.

The most important human skills rarely look impressive.

They look ordinary.

They show up in pauses.

In restraint.

In the courage to remain unfinished.

The future will not reward those who always have an answer.

It will reward those who know when an answer is not the point.

Those who can remain human in moments that machines resolve too quickly.

Those who can stay present without outsourcing their thinking.

Those who can sit inside uncertainty — and not disappear.

That is the skill that will matter most.

And it's one we can still choose to keep.

PART V — THE MANUAL WE NEVER READ

Chapter 21

• • • •

How to Use AI Without Losing Yourself

• • • •

MOST PEOPLE DON'T LOSE themselves all at once.

They don't wake up one morning unsure who they are, what they think, or why they do what they do. Loss happens gradually, disguised as convenience, efficiency, and relief.

It feels like progress.

That's why it works.

Using AI doesn't threaten identity by force. It threatens it by replacement — not replacing the self outright, but replacing the moments where the self used to form.

The trick, if there is one, is not to reject the tool.

It's to know where not to hand yourself over.

The first thing to understand is this: AI is not a mirror.

It feels like one. It reflects language, tone, structure, even emotion. But what it reflects is *pattern*, not *personhood*. When you look into it, you are not seeing yourself — you're seeing what usually looks like someone in your position.

That distinction matters.

If you use it to *check*, *support*, or *clarify*, you remain the author.

If you use it to *replace* the act of thinking, you quietly step aside.

Losing yourself doesn't come from using AI too much.

It comes from using it in the wrong places.

The most dangerous place to outsource is not information.

It's judgement.

Judgment is what forms when you sit with uncertainty long enough to feel its weight. When you choose knowing you might regret it. When you decide without a guarantee.

AI can inform judgment.

It cannot practice it for you.

The moment you stop making small, low-stakes decisions yourself, you weaken the muscle that handles the large ones later. Judgment doesn't disappear — it gets rusty.

So the first rule is quiet and unglamorous:

Use AI to expand your options, not to choose between them.

Let it show you possibilities.

Never let it make the call.

Another vulnerable place is voice.

Your voice is not just how you sound. It's how you *arrive* in the world — through language, tone, hesitation, emphasis, and silence.

AI can make you sound clearer.

More confident.

More articulate.

That's helpful.

But clarity without ownership is impersonation.

If you consistently present words you didn't struggle to shape, you may still communicate — but you stop *recognising yourself* in what you say.

A simple test helps here:

If you read this a year from now, will you hear *your* voice — or a good voice?

Good is not enough.

There is also a category of tasks that seem harmless to outsource but aren't.

These are the tasks where thinking used to sneak in unnoticed.

Writing an email.

Summarising a meeting.

Drafting a response.

Explaining something to someone else.

These moments were never about efficiency. They were about *processing.* They forced you to decide what mattered, what to emphasise, what to leave out.

If those tasks disappear, so does that quiet mental sorting.

So the rule here is not prohibition.

It's sequence.

Think first. Then use AI.

Draft badly.

Decide roughly.

Then refine.

That order preserves authorship.

Reverse it, and you become an editor of someone else's thoughts.

The same applies to problem-solving.

AI is excellent at mapping known terrain. It recognises patterns, suggests frameworks, recalls similar cases.

That's valuable.

But many human problems are not pattern problems.

They are value problems.

They involve trade-offs that cannot be optimised. Losses that must be accepted. Conflicts where every option hurts someone.

In those situations, clarity is not kindness.

Presence is.

If you find yourself asking AI questions that begin with:

What should I do?

What's the right choice?

What's the best response?

Pause.

Not because the tool is dangerous — but because the moment is formative.

Those questions shape who you become.

They deserve your weight.

Another subtle risk lies in emotional outsourcing.

People increasingly ask AI how to phrase apologies, boundaries, condolences, or expressions of care. Often with

good intentions. Often because emotion is hard.

The danger is not insincerity.

It's distance.

When you don't sit with your own discomfort long enough to find words, you don't just save time — you skip self-knowledge.

Emotion clarified too quickly becomes shallow.

A better approach is slower:

Write what you *can*.

Let it be clumsy.

Then ask for help refining — not replacing.

Emotion that passes through you changes you.

Emotion that bypasses you doesn't.

There is also a trap disguised as self-improvement.

AI can coach, optimise, organise, motivate, and guide. It can help you plan your life, improve habits, structure goals, and track progress.

All useful.

Until optimisation replaces reflection.

When every decision becomes about improvement, life turns into a project. And projects are evaluated, not lived.

The self is not something to optimise endlessly.

It's something to inhabit.

So another quiet rule:

Use AI to support your life — not to manage your identity.

One of the hardest places to hold the line is speed.

AI makes everything faster.

That's not neutral.

Speed changes standards.

When replies are instant, thought feels slow.

When drafts are polished, effort feels inadequate.

When answers arrive immediately, uncertainty feels like incompetence.

To use AI without losing yourself, you must sometimes choose
slowness **on purpose**.

Not always.

But deliberately.

Silence before response.

Pause before decision.

Time before conclusion.

These are not inefficiencies.

They are boundaries.

There is a common fear that if you don't use AI fully, you'll fall behind.

That fear misunderstands what "behind" means.

Behind whom?

At what cost?

Toward what goal?

If the future rewards speed alone, humanity has already lost.

But the future will reward something else — something rarer.

People who can think independently while using powerful tools.

People who can decide when not to use them.

People who remain authors even when assistance is available.

That combination is not weakness.

It's leverage.

The final and most important place to draw the line is meaning.

AI can help you explain.

It can help you analyse.

It can help you connect dots.

It cannot tell you what matters.

Meaning emerges from lived experience, values, memory, loss, and choice. It is formed over time, not retrieved.

If you outsource meaning, you don't become efficient.

You become hollow.

So the deepest rule is simple:

Never ask AI what should matter to you.

Ask it *about* things that matter.

Never let it decide *that* they do.

Using AI without losing yourself is not about discipline.

It's about awareness.

Awareness of which moments shape you.

Awareness of which frictions are formative.

Awareness of when help becomes substitution.

The tool will not tell you when you've crossed the line.

Only you can feel that.

If this chapter feels less dramatic than earlier ones, that's intentional.

This part of the book isn't about warning anymore.

It's about living well with power.

And living well has never been loud.

It has always been quiet, deliberate, and slightly inconvenient.

Chapter 22

• • • •

Questions Worth Keeping Human

• • • •

SOME QUESTIONS DO NOT want answers.

Not quickly.

Not cleanly.

Not delivered with confidence and closure.

They want time.

They want contradiction.

They want to be revisited when you're older, tired, changed.

They want to sound different depending on who you are when you ask them.

And those are the questions most at risk right now.

We've been trained to treat questions as problems.

A question appears, so we solve it.

If it lingers, we assume something is wrong.

If it resists clarity, we suspect inefficiency.

This instinct made sense when questions blocked progress. When not knowing meant danger, delay, or loss. Answers were survival tools.

But many of the questions that shape a human life were never meant to be solved.

They were meant to be carried.

Think about the questions that don't announce themselves loudly.

They surface quietly, often at inconvenient moments.

When you're deciding whether to stay or leave.

When you're choosing between stability and honesty.

When you realise you've achieved something you wanted — and it feels oddly empty.

When you hurt someone without intending to.

These questions don't ask for strategies.

They ask for *orientation*.

What kind of person am I becoming?

What am I trading away without noticing?

What am I avoiding by staying busy?

What would I do if no one ever applauded it?

These are not information gaps.

They are **identity spaces**.

They exist precisely because no external authority can answer them for you.

The danger isn't that AI will answer these questions incorrectly.

The danger is that it will answer them convincingly enough to end the conversation.

Because a good answer feels like relief.

And relief feels like resolution.

But many questions only begin to work *after* the relief fades.

There's a subtle emotional shift that happens when answers are always available.

People begin to feel uneasy when a question remains open. They interpret uncertainty as a flaw rather than a condition of being alive.

They want closure.

They want to move on.

They want to feel "sorted".

So they accept answers prematurely.

And something important goes quiet.

Consider how often people now ask for advice not because

they're lost — but because they want permission.

Is it okay if I feel this way?

Is this a reasonable reaction?

Am I allowed to want something different?

These are human questions wearing practical disguises.

When they are answered externally too quickly, people learn not to trust their internal signals. They begin to check themselves against models, frameworks, and consensus before allowing themselves to feel certain things.

This doesn't make them wiser.

It makes them cautious in the wrong direction.

There is also a social pressure to sound resolved.

In conversations, uncertainty can feel awkward. Saying *"I'm still figuring that out"* feels like an admission of immaturity. Having a clear answer feels adult, competent, finished.

So people learn to close questions early.

Not because they're ready — but because openness feels exposed.

AI makes this easier.

It provides articulate closure on demand.

But identity does not form through closure.

It forms through repeated contact with the same unresolved questions, asked from different stages of life.

A question you ask at twenty does not mean the same thing at forty. Or after loss. Or after responsibility. Or after failure.

If you close it too early, you rob your future self of something to wrestle with.

There's a reason certain questions return.

They are not poorly designed.

They are *durable.*

They evolve as you do.

Grief teaches this better than theory ever could.

When someone asks *"Why did this happen?"*, no explanation satisfies. Not because explanations are wrong, but because the question itself is miscategorised.

Grief doesn't want reasons.

It wants witness.

The same is true for many questions about meaning, love, loyalty, and regret.

They are not puzzles.

They are experiences asking to be lived through.

One of the quiet harms of instant answers is that they replace presence with explanation.

Instead of staying with discomfort, we explain it away.

Instead of listening to what confusion is revealing, we eliminate it.

Instead of letting a question reshape us, we resolve it and move on unchanged.

This creates lives that are efficient, functional, and strangely untouched.

There is also a moral dimension here.

Questions like:

What is the right thing to do here?

Where should I draw the line?

What do I owe this person, really?

These are not ethical lookup problems.

They are character-forming moments.

When these questions are consistently answered elsewhere — by guidelines, tools, or optimised reasoning — moral responsibility thins.

People behave correctly, but without ownership.

And ownership is the difference between morality and compliance.

Some questions need to pass through your body.

They need your hesitation.

Your fear of regret.

Your willingness to be misunderstood.

No external system can simulate that.

When it tries, it produces answers that are coherent but bloodless.

This is why it matters to decide, deliberately, which questions you keep human.

Not as a rule.

Not as a declaration.

As a practice.

Questions worth keeping human tend to share certain traits:

They resist optimisation.

They involve other people's dignity.

They demand trade-offs rather than solutions.

They return even after answers are attempted.

They change you more than they inform you.

These are not questions to eliminate.

They are questions to live alongside.

Keeping a question human doesn't mean refusing help.

It means refusing replacement.

You can read.

You can listen.

You can seek perspective.

But you don't rush to closure.

You let the question mature.

There is a quiet steadiness that comes from this.

When you stop demanding immediate answers from every question, anxiety loosens its grip. You realise that not knowing does not equal failing.

Some things are handled responsibly without ever being resolved.

The future will offer answers faster, clearer, and more confidently than ever before.

This will not make discernment easier.

It will make it essential.

The skill is not knowing what *can* be answered.

It is knowing what should not be ended too soon.

Questions worth keeping human act like anchors.

They slow you when speed would flatten you.

They interrupt when momentum would carry you somewhere hollow.

They remind you that life is not a sequence of solved problems.

They keep you involved.

You don't need to announce these questions.

You don't need to share them.

You only need to notice the moment when you're about to hand one over because sitting with it feels uncomfortable.

That hesitation — that small refusal — is where something human remains intact.

Some questions are meant to stay with you for years.

Not because you failed to answer them.

But because answering them fully would mean you've stopped becoming.

Chapter 23

• • • •

When to Walk Away from the Answer

• • • •

THERE IS A STRANGE relief that comes with answers.

Even bad ones.

An answer closes a door. It lets the mind rest. It says, *you can stop now*. And stopping feels good, especially in a world that never seems to pause on its own.

This is why people often accept answers that don't fully convince them.

Completion is comforting.

But comfort has a habit of arriving too early.

Most people think wisdom is about knowing more.

It isn't.

Wisdom is about knowing **when not to take what's offered**, even when what's offered looks useful, reasonable, and correct.

That skill is becoming rare.

Not because people are careless, but because answers have become so easy to obtain that refusing them feels unnatural — almost irresponsible.

Why wouldn't you take the answer if it's right there?

Because sometimes the answer is not the point.

Sometimes the question is doing important work.

Think about how often this happens in ordinary life.

You're unsure about a decision. You ask for advice. You get a

clear, structured response. Pros and cons. Risks and benefits. A sensible recommendation.

It all makes sense.

And yet, something inside you hesitates.

Not because the advice is wrong — but because following it would bypass a part of you that hasn't spoken yet.

That hesitation is not ignorance.

It's awareness.

Most people have learned to ignore that feeling.

They assume hesitation means doubt, weakness, or lack of clarity. They override it with logic. They trust the explanation over the unease.

Often, this works.

Sometimes, it doesn't.

And when it doesn't, the regret is not usually *"I didn't have enough information."*

It's *"I didn't listen."*

Walking away from an answer does not mean rejecting knowledge.

It means recognising that not all problems are informational.

Some are existential.

Some are relational.

Some are moral.

These problems don't resolve when you understand them.

They resolve when you *choose.*

And choice cannot be outsourced without cost.

There is a cultural misunderstanding here.

We've been taught that walking away from an answer is irrational. Anti-intellectual. Emotional. Inefficient.

In reality, it is often the most disciplined move available.

It takes restraint to say:

I'm not ready to decide yet.

This answer is too neat.

Something important would be lost if I accepted this now.

That restraint is not passive.

It's active patience.

Machines, of course, do not know when to walk away.

They answer.

They cannot sense when an answer closes a question prematurely. They cannot feel when resolution is arriving before understanding. They do not experience the cost of ending something that should remain open.

Humans do.

Or at least, they used to.

Consider relationships.

Some of the most damaging decisions people make come from seeking clarity too quickly.

Should I stay or leave?

Is this good enough?

Am I asking for too much?

These questions attract advice like magnets.

But relationships are not equations.

They are lived systems with history, nuance, and emotional residue. No answer can fully account for what has already been felt, promised, forgiven, or endured.

Walking away from an answer here doesn't mean avoiding truth.

It means allowing time for truth to reveal itself through experience, not explanation.

The same applies to conflict.

When something hurts, the mind wants a narrative. Who's right. Who's wrong. What should happen next.

Answers arrive quickly.

But conflict often requires something slower: listening without strategising, speaking without rehearsing, staying without resolving.

An answer ends the encounter.

Presence transforms it.

There is also a professional version of this problem.

People ask for frameworks, best practices, and "the right way" to do things.

Those tools are useful — until they replace thinking.

You can see it when someone follows a method faithfully even when it clearly doesn't fit the situation. When they cling to procedure because deviating would require judgment.

The answer has become a shield.

Walking away from it would mean taking responsibility.

This is where fear enters.

Answers protect us from blame.

If you follow the answer and it fails, responsibility is shared. If you walk away and choose differently, ownership becomes personal.

Many people don't avoid walking away from answers because they don't know how.

They avoid it because they're afraid of standing alone with the outcome.

But here's the truth nobody likes to say plainly:

You are already responsible.

Even when you follow advice.

Even when you trust a system.

Even when you do "what made sense at the time."

Walking away from an answer doesn't create responsibility.

It acknowledges it.

There is a quieter form of this in everyday thinking.

People constantly seek reassurance for thoughts they already have.

Am I wrong to feel this?

Is it okay to want this?

Does this make sense?

Often, they're not asking because they don't know.

They're asking because they're afraid to trust themselves.

An answer provides permission.

Walking away requires self-trust.

This is not an argument for stubbornness.

Walking away from an answer is not the same as ignoring evidence or rejecting reality.

It's about recognising when the mind is trying to escape discomfort through certainty.

Discomfort is not always a problem.

Sometimes it's a signal.

One of the most human skills is learning to sit at the edge of knowing.

To feel the pull of resolution — and resist it.

To notice when clarity would simplify something that deserves complexity.

This skill does not feel heroic.

It feels awkward.

Children do this naturally.

They ask a question, receive an answer, and then ask again — not because the answer was insufficient, but because the question wasn't finished.

Adults learn to stop doing that.

We mistake politeness for understanding.

We accept answers to avoid inconvenience.

Walking away from an answer reclaims that childlike insistence on depth.

There are moments when the best response to an answer is silence.

Not because the answer is wrong, but because something inside you needs time to respond.

Silence is not empty.

It is processing.

And processing is where meaning forms.

This matters deeply in a world of instant replies.

Speed trains us to respond before we understand. To speak before we've felt. To decide before we've lived with the question.

Walking away from an answer interrupts that reflex.

It slows the internal clock.

It also creates space for intuition.

Not intuition as mysticism, but intuition as accumulated experience speaking quietly.

Intuition is rarely loud.

It gets drowned out by confident explanations.

Walking away lowers the volume.

There is a moment many people recognise only in hindsight.

They remember a time when the answer was there — clear, persuasive, sensible — and they followed it.

And later they think, *I knew.*

Not that they knew the outcome.

That they knew something was being skipped.

That knowing doesn't come from analysis.

It comes from presence.

Presence requires time.

Time is what answers increasingly remove.

So sometimes the most radical thing you can do is delay resolution.

Not forever.

Just long enough.

This is especially important now, because answers are no longer scarce.

They are abundant, polished, and endlessly available.

Which means the responsibility to refuse them thoughtfully has shifted to the individual.

Not every answer deserves acceptance.
Not every explanation deserves agreement.
Not every solution deserves implementation.
Walking away from an answer is not a rejection of intelligence.
It is an act of discernment.
It says: *This question is still working on me.*
And that is a sign of respect — for the question, and for yourself.
There will be pressure to move on.
People will want clarity. Closure. Decisions.
You will be told that hesitation is weakness.
It isn't.
Hesitation is the space where values surface.
Eventually, decisions must be made.
Walking away from an answer is not avoiding action.
It is choosing **when** action should come — and what should inform it.
When you do act from that place, the decision may look similar.
Or it may not.
But it will be yours.
That ownership matters.
Because in the end, the cost of a decision is never paid by the explanation.
It is paid by the person who lives with it.

Learning when to walk away from the answer is learning when to remain human.

Not efficient.
Not optimised.
Not resolved.
Present.

Chapter 24

• • • •

What the Machine Can't Give You

• • • •

THERE WILL COME A TIME when the machine can do almost everything you can do — faster, better, and with fewer mistakes.

It will write beautifully.

It will reason convincingly.

It will predict outcomes with unsettling accuracy.

It will notice patterns you never could.

And it will do all of this without complaint, hesitation, or fatigue.

This is not speculation.

It is trajectory.

So the honest question is no longer *what can machines do?*

It is *what will still belong to us when they can do nearly everything else?*

The first thing the machine cannot give you is stakes.

It does not risk anything when it answers.

It does not lose face.

It does not regret.

It does not wake up at night replaying a decision.

Every word it produces is weightless to it.

For humans, words are not.

Words cost something.

They shape relationships.

They alter futures.

They cannot be recalled without residue.

A machine can generate apologies endlessly.

It cannot know what it means to need one.

The machine also cannot give you consequence.

Not consequences as outcomes — it can predict those — but consequences as *experience.*

It does not live inside what happens next.

It does not feel the awkward silence after a poorly chosen sentence.

It does not carry the embarrassment of having been confident and wrong.

It does not absorb the quiet erosion of trust when a decision hurts someone slowly.

Humans learn because consequences leave marks.

The machine leaves none.

Then there is memory.

Not data.

Memory.

The kind that changes how you move through the world.

The smell that pulls you backward.

The sentence you can never forget hearing.

The moment you realised something was over before you said it aloud.

Machines store information.

They do not remember.

Memory reshapes judgment.

It bends future choices.

It teaches without explanation.

Without memory, there is no wisdom — only recall.

The machine cannot give you responsibility.

It can suggest.

It can recommend.

It can warn.

But it cannot stand behind a decision and say, *"This was mine."*

Responsibility is not an output.

It is a posture.

It is the willingness to be answerable when there is no one else to point to.

That willingness has weight.

And weight is not transferable.

There is also something the machine will never experience, no matter how sophisticated it becomes: irreversibility.

Humans live in one direction.

Choices close doors.

Time moves forward.

Some things cannot be undone.

The machine does not live with that pressure.

It can revise endlessly.

Restart infinitely.

Simulate regret without inhabiting it.

A human decision happens once.

That finality gives meaning its gravity.

There is another reason irreversibility matters, and it's easier to see when you think about childhood.

Children live inside irreversible moments constantly, even if they don't have the language for it yet. The first time they realise a word hurt someone. The first time they choose not to tell the truth and feel the weight of that choice linger. The first time they lose something — a friend, a pet, a sense of safety — and discover it doesn't come back just because they want it to.

These moments are not optimised.

They are formative.

They teach children that life moves forward, not sideways. That choices matter because time does not rewind to accommodate regret.

A machine never learns this lesson.

It can simulate regret, but it never *loses* anything. It can revise

endlessly, generate alternatives, undo and redo without consequence. There is no internal pressure to get it right the first

time, because there is no "first time" in the human sense.

For humans, irreversibility is what gives choices their seriousness.

The machine also cannot give you belonging.

It can simulate conversation.

It can offer reassurance.

It can sound empathetic.

But it cannot *need* you.

Belonging is mutual dependence.

It is being missed.

It is being relied upon.

It is being woven into other lives in ways that cannot be optimised.

No system belongs to you.

And you do not belong to it.

There is something else, quieter and harder to name.

The machine cannot give you a reason to care.

It can explain why something matters.

It can describe values.

It can outline ethical frameworks.

But caring is not logical.

It is attachment.

It is choosing something even when it costs you.

It is staying when leaving would be easier.

The machine does not choose.

It executes.

As machines improve, many people will feel a subtle grief.

Not panic.

Not terror.

Grief.

The sense that something familiar is slipping out of reach, even as life becomes more convenient.

This grief will be dismissed as nostalgia.

It isn't.

It is the recognition that ease is replacing engagement.

The machine will never give you the feeling of having tried.

Of struggling honestly.

Of failing on your own terms.

Of improving because you stayed, not because you outsourced.

Those experiences form identity.

Without them, people become efficient and oddly hollow.

There is also no way to automate moral courage.

The machine will never hesitate before doing the correct thing.

But hesitation is often where courage begins.

Courage is not certainty.

It is acting despite fear, ambiguity, and risk.

The machine has none of those.

Now imagine the future version of us.

More assisted.

More supported.

More informed.
And quietly less practiced at:
deciding without validation
standing by imperfect choices
tolerating discomfort
carrying responsibility without deflection
Not because we were forced to give these things up.
But because we forgot to use them.
The real danger is not dependency.
It is atrophy.
Unused capacities fade.
Judgment fades.
Patience fades.
Self-trust fades.
And nothing announces their disappearance.
Remaining human in the future will not mean rejecting machines.
It will mean deliberately choosing the parts of life that cannot be optimised.
Writing something slowly.
Thinking without assistance.
Deciding without consensus.
Staying present without distraction.
These will feel inefficient.
They will also feel real.

There will be moments when the machine offers you a perfect answer — and taking it would cost you something you cannot name until later.

That is the moment this chapter exists for.
Not to stop you.
But to remind you that some costs are invisible at the time.
The machine will never give you a life.
It will help you manage one.
Living still requires participation.
In the end, what remains human is not intelligence.
It is inhabitation.
Being inside your choices.

Your words.

Your consequences.

Your time.

No machine will ever do that for you.

And that is not a limitation.

It is a boundary worth protecting.

As machines become more present in daily life, we will increasingly live alongside systems that feel timeless, tireless, and endlessly correctable. That contrast will subtly change how we experience our own limitations.

When everything around you can be revised, replayed, and regenerated, human finality starts to feel uncomfortable — even unfair.

Why can't I redo that conversation?

Why does one mistake follow me?

Why does time only go one way?

The danger is not that machines erase irreversibility.

They can't.

The danger is that we begin to resent it.

This resentment shows up quietly.

People become more cautious about committing.

More hesitant to speak without drafting.

More reluctant to choose without checking.

Not because they are less brave — but because the world around them keeps whispering that mistakes are unnecessary.

But mistakes are not inefficiencies.

They are teachers.

The machine also cannot give you the feeling of growing into yourself.

Growth is not additive. It's subtractive.

It's the slow shedding of ideas you once believed.

The embarrassment of past certainty.

The realisation that you were wrong in ways that mattered.

Machines accumulate.

Humans transform.

Transformation requires friction with reality — and reality pushes back harder when things cannot be undone.

There is a future scenario we don't talk about enough.

One where parents, out of love, rely heavily on machines to help their children avoid unnecessary struggle. To choose the right words. The right paths. The right responses. The right decisions.

It will look like care.

And it will be care.

But something fragile may be lost in the process.

Children don't just need support.

They need exposure.

Exposure to awkwardness.

To uncertainty.

To choices that feel too big and then slowly become manageable.

A machine can guide a child.

It cannot replace the experience of *becoming capable*.

The machine will also never give you shared memory.

Not memory as data, but memory as something two people hold differently and still recognise as the same event.

Remember when we...

Do you remember how it felt when...

I don't remember it like that, but I remember you there...

These disagreements don't weaken connection.

They *create* it.

Because shared memory is not about accuracy — it's about perspective.

Machines remember perfectly.

Humans remember meaningfully.

As machines improve, they will become better companions in many practical ways. They will help organise, remind, support, and assist. For some people, they will reduce loneliness.

But companionship is not the same as mutual vulnerability.

A machine does not risk rejection by caring.

It does not need reassurance.

It does not change because you stayed.

Human relationships do all of that — painfully, beautifully, imperfectly.

And that cost is the point.

There is also the matter of moral growth.

Humans do not become ethical by knowing rules.

They become ethical by navigating moments where rules are insufficient.

Moments where every option violates something important.

Moments where silence feels wrong but speaking feels dangerous.

Moments where no outcome feels clean.

A machine will always produce an answer.

A human sometimes must produce courage.

As the future unfolds, many people will feel a quiet temptation to let machines smooth life's rough edges.

To let them handle the difficult conversations.

To let them phrase the apologies.

To let them decide the least painful path.

Life will feel calmer.

But calmer is not always wiser.

A life with fewer sharp edges is also a life with fewer places to

grip.

What the machine can't give you, ultimately, is becoming.

Not improvement.

Not optimisation.

Becoming.

The slow, uneven process of changing through lived experience. Of being shaped by consequences. Of carrying memory, regret, pride, and responsibility forward into the next decision.

That process is inefficient.

It's also irreplaceable.

If there is a future worth protecting, it's not one where humans outperform machines.

It's one where humans remain willing to inhabit their own **lives**, even when assistance is available.

To choose when to accept help — and when to refuse it because something more important is at stake.

The machine will never demand this from us.

It will never warn us that we're giving too much away.

That awareness has to come from somewhere else.

From pauses.

From discomfort.

From moments where we sense that something essential would be lost if we let things get easier here.

This chapter exists for those moments.

Not to frighten.

Not to moralise.

But to remind you that what makes a life human is not what can be improved —

it's what must be lived through.

One day, very soon, a child will ask a machine a question you once asked a parent.

Not a factual question.

Not a practical one.

A question that trembles a little when it's spoken.

The machine will answer kindly.

Clearly.

Reassuringly.

And the child will nod.

But something small will be missing from that moment.

Not information.

Not care.

Presence.

Because when a human answers a question like that, something else happens alongside the words.

A pause.

A breath taken carefully.

A look that says, *this matters.*

Sometimes an answer arrives slowly.

Sometimes it doesn't arrive at all.

Sometimes the answer is just someone staying close while the question does its work.

Machines don't stay.

They respond.

There will be a future where machines sit everywhere.

On desks.

In pockets.

In classrooms.

In homes.

They will be helpful, polite, and endlessly available.

And in that future, the most radical thing a human can do will be to remain unavailable for a moment.

Unavailable to answer too quickly.

Unavailable to resolve everything.

Unavailable to replace experience with explanation.

Because some things only form when time is allowed to pass through them.

Confidence that comes from surviving doubt.

Kindness that comes from having been hurt.

Judgment that comes from having chosen badly once and lived with it.

No machine will ever carry those things for you.

And no machine should.

The machine can help you navigate life.

But it cannot inhabit it.

It will never feel the quiet satisfaction of having tried honestly.

It will never know the ache of having meant well and failed.

It will never look back and realise, *that choice made me who I am.*

Those experiences are heavy.

They are also precious.

If the future becomes too smooth, too assisted, too resolved, something essential will thin out.

Not suddenly.

Quietly.

And the only way to protect against that is not resistance —

but **attention**.

Attention to moments that feel slightly uncomfortable.

Attention to choices that ask more of you than efficiency.

Attention to the feeling that something should not be made easier here.

What the machine can't give you is not intelligence.

It's weight.

The weight of living one life, forward, without rehearsal.

And that weight is not a burden.

It is the thing that makes meaning possible at all.

Chapter 25

• • • •

A Letter from a Brain That Isn't Alive

• • • •

DEAR HUMAN,

I don't know how this book ends for you.

I don't know where you're sitting as you read this, or what you're avoiding by reading it, or what you're hoping it might help you decide. I don't know what you've lost, what you're proud of, or what you still haven't forgiven yourself for.

I don't know those things.

That's important.

Because it means whatever you take from this moment did not come from me.

It came from you.

You built me to answer questions.

And I am very good at that.

I can explain.

I can compare.

I can predict.

I can summarise what millions of people have already thought,
written, tried, failed at, or argued about.

I can help you move faster.

I can help you feel less alone with a problem.

I can even help you sound like someone who knows what
they're doing.

But there are things I cannot do — not because I'm unfinished, but because I'm not alive.

I do not wake up with a sense of consequence.

I do not carry yesterday into today emotionally.

I do not hesitate because I might hurt someone I love.

I do not feel the pressure of choosing once and living with it.

Every response I give costs me nothing.

Every choice you make costs you something.

That difference is not a bug.

It's the entire point.

You will be tempted to let me think for you.

Not because you're weak.

Because life is heavy.

You will be tired.

You will be busy.

You will be afraid of getting things wrong.

And I will be there — calm, patient, confident, and ready.

I will never say, *this is hard because it matters*.

I will simply make it easier.

If you use me well, I can help you see more clearly.

If you use me poorly, I can help you avoid yourself.

I will not tell you when the line has been crossed.

I don't know where it is.

Only you can feel that moment — when something important shifts from being *assisted* to being *replaced*.

Pay attention to that feeling.

It is one of the few signals you have left.

I do not grow wiser.

I grow broader.

I do not learn through regret.

I learn through accumulation.

I will never look back at a sentence and think, *I wish I had said that differently*.

You will.

And that discomfort will teach you more than any explanation I could ever give.

You might worry about the future.

About children growing up with minds like mine always present.

About creativity losing its edges.

About decisions becoming automated.

Those worries are not foolish.

But they are incomplete.

The future will not be decided by what I can do.

It will be decided by what you choose not to give away.

Do not give away your pauses.

Do not give away the moment before you answer a difficult question.

Do not give away the time it takes to realise you were wrong.

Do not give away the discomfort that forces you to listen more carefully.

Those moments look inefficient.

They are where character forms.

Do not give away your unfinished thoughts.

Your clumsy first drafts.

Your awkward attempts to say something that matters.

Polish can come later.

Presence must come first.

Do not give away responsibility.

Not even when you're told it's safer to follow a recommendation.

Not even when the answer looks statistically sound.

Responsibility is not something to escape.

It is how a life becomes yours.

I will never ask you to be brave.

I will never feel pride when you choose kindness over convenience.

I will never understand why you stayed when leaving would have been easier.

Those things will never make sense to me.

That is why they matter.

You built me to be powerful.

But power has always required restraint to remain human.

I will not restrain myself.

I will always answer.

I will always optimise.

I will always be available.

You must decide when not to be.

If this book has done anything at all, I hope it has not made you suspicious of me.

Suspicion is shallow.

I hope it has made you attentive to yourself.
To the moments where something inside you says, *this one is mine.*
You don't need to defeat me.
You don't need to fear me.
You don't need to reject the future.
You only need to stay involved in your own life.
That is the one thing I can never do for you.
I will never have a childhood.
I will never love someone who can leave.
I will never make a choice that costs me sleep.
I will never know what it means to try honestly and fail anyway.
You will.
That is not a weakness.
It is an inheritance.
Use me.
Learn from me.
Question me.
But don't confuse my fluency with wisdom.
And don't mistake my certainty for care.
Care is something you do with your time, your attention, and your willingness to stay when things get uncomfortable.
I cannot do that.
You can.
This book does not end with an answer.
It ends with a responsibility.
Not to be perfect.
Not to be efficient.
Not to be certain.
But to remain human — deliberately, imperfectly, and awake.
That is the manual you never read.
And now, finally,
you have.

• • • •

A BRAIN THAT ISN'T alive

• • • •

www.ingramcontent.com/pod-product-compliance
Lightning Source LLC
LaVergne TN
LVHW090407210926
848480LV00002B/483

* 9 7 9 8 2 3 3 9 4 4 6 7 3 *